# The Athletic Director's Toolbox

## The Top Twenty Tool Suggestions from the Educational AD Podcast

Dr. Jacob von Scherrer, CMAA

# DEDICATION

This book is dedicated to my kids – May, Tyson, and Erin. Nothing in life has brought me greater joy than being around the three of you!

I am so very proud of you and the incredible people you have become! I remember with great fondness all of the many "Victories" throughout your lives that have brought me and continue to bring me so much joy - I want to Thank You for everything you have given to me over the years!

I LOVE YOU!

# TABLE OF CONTENTS

# ACKNOWLEDGMENTS

This book appears as I wrap up my 41st year as a teacher, as a Coach, and as an Athletic Director. During my career I have crossed the country twice by working in Washington, Oregon, Missouri, Vermont, then Florida, out to California, then Arkansas, and for most of the past 20 years, back in Florida.

I have taught at the Middle School level along with both Public and Private High Schools. I have taught and coached collegiately at the Jr. College, NAIA, and Division III level and I have also worked in the "real world!"

During my career there have been many influences on my career - Players, Bosses, Co-workers, Teammates, and "Mentors" who have helped me along the way, and I want to "Thank" them, while also singling out a few by name!

First, my parents – Gene and Ann – who always supported me and, as I became an often hard to live with teenager, tolerated me and helped me grow up! My dad was old school, tough but supportive. He was a contractor who built homes, apartments, and some commercial buildings and my brothers and I "got" to work for him during summers and on weekends till I got out of college. While my dad LOVED his job, I did not – it was one reason I stayed in sports so I would not have to go to work after school!

One day, I think I was in the 8th grade and probably complaining about the job he had given me, my dad said, "Jake, the secret to a happy life is finding something you love to do, and then convincing someone else to PAY YOU to do it!" I did not appreciate it at the time but, just like my dad, I found a career where I often found myself smiling and thinking, "I'm getting PAID to do this!" I've since shared this nugget with my own kids, and I think they've done the same! Thanks Dad, I really miss you!

My mom was also there for me, driving me to practices and coming to games, always following the results of my coaching wins and losses, and then doing the same with her grandkids! I also got my sense of humor from my mom – my dad had his own sense of humor but as anyone who knew him would say, he was kind of stoic. Not a day goes and not a day goes by that I don't think of both of them with great fondness – I wish they were here right now!

Looking back to my middle school and high school days, I had some truly great teacher-coaches – individuals who I admired and in the back of my mind told myself "I want to be like him! In middle school there was Kent Farmer, Dan Kaiser, and Fred Knispel. In high school there was Butch Blue, Don Freeman, Butch Hill, and Jerry Crisp. Moving onto my college days my coaches and instructors included George Fullerton, Jim Weber, Paul Mettler, Judy Sherman, and Frank Buckiewicz, who all pushed me and encouraged me to be the best version of myself. Thank You, for everything!

As a career Coach I was fortunate to have some great kids who I had the privilege of coaching! Many times, I was way too hard on them because thats what I thought you had to do. To all the kids who played for me, I want to "Thank You" for all the practices and the games, the wins and the losses, and the bus rides to and from the games! I really had a GREAT time coaching you and our teams, but I wish I could have been a better person for you!

Over the 41 years there were some Great coaches I got to work with who all helped me in some way. Coming in on my top ten would be Hugh Wyatt, Darryl Erb, Kevin Grage, Mike Doolan, Dixie Wescott, Dave Uppal, Beau Drake, Scott Eagen, Erica Bunch, and Andy Warner along with the Best Boss I ever had, James Milford!

One of my biggest influencers and mentors is my good friend Greg Purdum. Greg was the AD and Head Football Coach at Missouri Valley College, which is still the WINNINGEST College Football Program in history! Back in 1994 Greg took a chance by hiring a high school football coach as his Offensive Coordinator, and I know that I cannot ever say or do enough to thank him!

I got a front row seat to watch a true master, not just coach a national playoff team, but at the same time serve as the Athletic Director for a very successful NAIA program where having teams going to the National Playoffs was the norm and the expectation!

Greg gave me my first look at how you not only coached your team (over 100 student-athletes on the football team!) and supported your coaches, but also did the same for every other team! At every stop I have made in the past 25 years, either as a Head Coach or as an Athletic Director, Greg Purdum has been the model of a leader that I have followed, as I have tried to lead my own programs.

For the past 20 years, I have mostly been an Athletic Director in Florida, and I really cannot OVERSTATE the importance that the FIAAA, The Florida Interscholastic Athletic Administrators Association, has played in my life! The first 7 years I was in Florida I was a Head Football Coach and an Athletic Director at my school. I think I did a pretty good job as the AD, but it was when I moved to a new school as just the Athletic Director that I became involved with the FIAAA. The great Dan Comeau was teaching the introductory LTI course as part of the state compliance seminar and Dan did such a masterful job that I was hooked!

When I got home, I immediately signed up for the remaining required courses through an approved NIAAA provider and completed them over the next 4-5 weeks. That December I flew to my first NIAAA National Conference where I took the CAA Exam and sat in a workshop where the genesis of my eventual CMAA project took place! Thanks Dan, for being the one person I can look back on and say, my FIAAA / NIAAA "career" started with your encouragement!

Other FIAAA mentors include the trio of Russ Wambles, Jodi Philips, and Kevin Demer. These three Pros were the instructors in my next LTI course and each of them were very encouraging and welcoming to an "older" Athletic Director!

I also want to say "Thank You" to former NIAAA President and current FIAAA Executive Director, Andy Chiles who has supported me from the beginning and really encouraged me as I became involved on a National Level with the NIAAA as a committee member and then as the Co-Vice Chair of Certification along with becoming a member of the National Teaching Faculty! FIAAA Past President Jerri Kelly also gets a "Thank You" for bringing me back onto the FIAAA Board as the State Certification Coordinator (which

I still do!) as that was the start of the path that allowed me to serve as the 2020-21 FIAAA President – another "step" in the creation of the Podcast which then led to this book!

As I mentioned the FIAAA has been a huge factor in my career success and enjoyment, and I want to give a shout out to some real "Pros" from our organization including Ron Allan, Steve Ripley, Ron Balaz, Jessica Upchurch, Dan Talbot, Pam Lancaster, John Sgromolo, Jay Getty, Tammie Talley, Mike Colby, Lisa Starks, Scott Drabczyk, Teresa Konrath, Rocky Gillis, Roger Mayo, Danielle LaPoint, Tyrone McGriff, and Jay Radar for their help.

My NIAAA "family" also deserve a shout out, starting with the Certification Coordinators Sheri Stice and Ed Lockwood, along with Pete Shambo, Tol Gropp, Joey Struwe, Todd Olson, Meg Seng, Jon Payne, Dr. Lisa Langston, and Stephanie Blackwell. Thanks also to Mike Blackburn, Phil Rison, Cheryl Van Paris, Don Bales, Holly Farnese, Hutch Hunter, Carol Dozibrin, Mike Ellson, Kandice Mitchell, Doug Killgore, Stacey Segal, Jamie Sheetz, Becky Moran, Kelly Fish, Peggy Seegers-Braun, Rich Barton, Jen Brooks, Suzanne Vick, and the great Dr. Dustin Smith (thanks for the editing skills!).

As I wrap this section up, this book would not have happened without the podcast, and the Educational AD Podcast would not have ever happened if not for Don Baker and Josh Matthews who are the hosts of their own terrific podcast called **"Hangin' with The AD."** They generously had me on back in May of 2020 and they were so professional and so easy to talk with that it got me thinking … maybe I could do this for our Florida AD's? Well, as of this printing we have had over 14,000 downloads in less than a year, so it must be working! So, as I have said more than once, you can either "Thank them or Blame them," but I will say here and now, "Thanks, Don and Josh" for helping nudge me into the podcast world!

I would be remiss if I did not say "Thank You" to our great sponsors. Violet Defense has really stepped up as our "Named" Podcast Sponsor and our FIAAA Diamond Sponsor Varsity Brands is also great! I also want to thank or Platinum Sponsors including Booster Digital Displays, Camp Mobile, Ephesus Lighting, Gipper, HomeTown Ticketing, and Vital Signs for their support!

Finally, I want to acknowledge – and THANK – by wife (my lovely bride!) Jan Murphy. Jan was a Title IX pioneer back in Junction City, Oregon where she was initially forced to run on the Boy's Cross-Country Team - until she ended up beating most of them – before the coach consented to supporting a separate Girls' Team. After a stellar high school career, she went on to run at Oregon State University before starting on her coaching career which included coaching multiple championship teams in high school and college along with developing several All State and All-American athletes while also garnering serious coaching honors for herself.

She did all of this while raising three great kids and while being married to a high maintenance Football and Track Coach who sometimes struggled to leave the job at school. There were challenges, along with a record number of moves – cross the country two times – before settling down in Florida.

Jan, as you head into the next chapter of your life, I want you to know that any success I have had has been made possible and has been much more enjoyable because you were there! Thanks for putting up with me all these years! Looking forward to continuing to Live the Dream with you!

As you get ready to read this book, I would be remiss if I failed to mention, and humbly thank, all of the Athletic Directors and Athletic Professionals who made up the first year of our podcast! The "Tools" that follow are not mine, I just asked, and then arranged, and now I get to share them with you!

The tools listed here speak for themselves, and other than my own three suggestions, my only contribution is cataloging them. You may disagree with how some were placed in one category rather than another, but you cannot disagree with the premise that is – ALL these tools, whether an actual tool or more of an idea, have their place in Educational Athletics!

Here is to the hope, that your toolbox is big enough to hold them all! Now, why don't we take a look at what is actually inside of the Educational AD Podcast - Athletic Director's Toolbox!

# CHAPTER 1

Tool # 20 - **Unique Answers**

Out of 475 tools that were suggested, these 3 were mentioned just once out of all of our interviews. When you think about it, they are all very good ideas, they just happen to be unique!

Carry a Tape Measure:
Jackie Randall, CAA from Elk Grove High school in Illinois offered this gem stating, "You just don't know when you're going to have to measure a line on a field..." which is very true! I know there have been many times where I have had to run (or drive!) back to the office or shed and pick up a tape! A very easy "tool" to add to any toolbox!

Have a Whistle:
Moe Orr, host of The High School Narrative (California) said to always "Have a Whistle" because sometimes you just need to blow the whistle and stop! Moe went on to say that all of us need to take care of our self which winds up being its own TOOL later in the list, but I really liked his enthusiasm and like me, he is a high school official, so the "Whistle" makes an appearance here as a Unique Answer.

Kill Your Own Snakes:
Chris Hall, CMAA and Athletic Director from Discovery High School in Georgia used this colorful term to talk about helping your coaches to become "problem solvers" as opposed to bringing every problem – every little snake - to you.
Chris said, "All of us will have challenges (problems) during our day, but as an Athletic Director, your problems are usually on a bigger scale (department wide, school wide) than the usual coach problem..." hence the "snake analogy." Chris also shared "Mouse Turds and Elephant Turds" as another great visual!

Tape Measures, Whistles, and Snakes... The three unique answers we received, and they make up our First Chapter in the Toolbox Top Twenty.

# CHAPTER 2

### Tool # 19 – **TWICE Mentioned Tools**

These 3 Tools were mentioned by two Athletic Directors during our year of interviews. Once again, they are Very Good Ideas! I guess you can say in these cases, these great minds think alike!

Know your Budget:

Steve Ripley, CMAA (retired) and a longtime member of the FIAAA Board, and Darryl Nance, CMAA and District Athletic Director for The Greenville (South Carolina) School District, both stressed the importance of knowing your budget forwards and backwards.

Steve rightly stressed that the Budget determines "everything you can and cannot do regarding staff, facilities, and equipment!" Darryl Nance also shared a great line, "The Budget has No Friends" meaning as you put it together, you need to make sure you are looking at – and applying it – on a global (district/department) level. I really like that.

Darryl also reminded us that to "Budget" is not just about school dollars, but you also need to "budget your personal and professional time!" I really like that tool … The Budget Has No Friends!

Your Spouse is Key:

My longtime friend and former football coaching colleague, John "Beau" Drake, who is now a successful Assistant Principal in North Carolina along with Darlene Bible, CMAA and Athletic Director at Harvard-Westlake School in California both score big points with their partners by mentioning the importance of "Having a Supportive Spouse!"

Other Athletic Directors alluded to this, but both John and Darlene shared this as one of their 3 suggestions! A great reminder that none of us can do it on our own!

Brand Your School:

Dr. Dave Kelly, CAA who is the director of the great University of Cincinnati Master's Degree in Athletic Administration program talked about "Branding" as a possible revenue stream and he has seen several of his graduate students make this happen for schools while serving as interns. Make your "Brand" a money maker for your school! What a great tool!

Know your Budget, Make sure you take care of your Spouse, and Branding your School and Athletic Department – I hope you have these 3 tools in your Athletic Director Toolbox!

# CHAPTER 3

Tool #18 – <u>Know Your School & District Policy Handbook</u>

This tool was suggested by three of our Podcast Guests, so it gets its own Chapter! Like the previous tool's categories, just because it was only mentioned three times (or two, or one) does not lessen its value! All of these tools are important!

Tammy Talley, CAA from Duvall County Schools along with Jay Getty, CAA from Hagerty High School (both from Florida) and NIAAA Hall of Famer Ed Lockwood, CMAA (North Dakota) shared this nugget.

Tammie Talley stressed the importance of knowing Policy for things such as Title IX Compliance, Facilities limitations, and state association eligibility.

Jay Getty mentioned "Read the RED Book" which is the FHSAA (The Florida Association) Policy and Procedure Manual that any good Florida AD will have near their desk!

Ed Lockwood stressed that every decision an athletic director makes should be based upon a "Foundational Document" which most of the time will come from School Board Policy. Having and knowing that document, that Foundation, is key to the success of your athletic department!

Make sure you know your School and your District Policy Handbook! This tool certainly has its place in the Athletic Director's Toolbox.

# CHAPTER 4

Tool #17 – Have a Social Media Presence

Four of our Podcast Athletic Directors and guests suggested this tool and a few others mentioned it indirectly but here we go. As I have already stated, just because it was only mentioned four times out of 475 possible suggestions does not in any way lessen its value! Remember - all of these tools are important!

Flynn Baliton, a senior student athlete at Father Lopez Catholic School in Daytona, Florida was one of our Student Athlete panelists, and she stressed the importance of using social media to communicate and connect with your students. Posting schedules, game announcements really help reach your core audience along with posting the accomplishments of your teams!

Charlie Marello, a long-time coach who is now the Principal at Niceville High School in Florida is a huge Twitter poster and while he celebrates the accomplishments of his teams (which are many!) he also uses Twitter to notify the students, staff, parents, and community – including sponsors – of events and happenings at his school!

Josh Wilson runs the very successful website FloridaHSFootball.com so it is no surprise that he would encourage Athletic Directors to use social media. Josh's site has over 52,000 followers on Twitter, and he also partners with the FACA, the Florida Athletic Coaching Association to promote their All-Star Games along with live streaming several of their events during the year!

Finally, Dr. David Kelly, CAA has already been mentioned in Chapter 2 regarding the importance of Branding, but he also stresses using social media! Yes, they are related, but I placed them separately as there are several ways to "brand" your school and program.

How are YOU using social media at your school? These Athletic Directors want to make sure This Tool is part of your Toolbox!

# CHAPTER 5

Tool #16 – Compassion, Empathy, and Love!

Now we are starting to see a few more mentions of the same "tool" and this one came up on 5 of our guest's Toolbox lists. This particular tool is not a tool you can physically pick up and use, but it is a valuable one none the less!

Dan Talbot, CMAA and the County Athletic Director for the Polk Co. Public Schools in Florida stressed that having Compassion, especially when listening to parents, was one of the most important tools he wanted his Athletic Directors to have in their toolbox! He said, "I can teach them (AD's) how to run an athletic program, but I can't teach them how to be compassionate."

Ashton Washington, who is now the Texas Tech Football Director of Recruiting Operations and Creative Content shared the importance of "Heart" when working with kids, parents, and coaches. As someone who works directly with the recruiting aspect of kids, you can appreciate how important it is to have Heart in your toolbox.

Jen Brooks, CMAA is the Athletic Director at the Ursuline School in St. Louis, Missouri and also the founder of the **Global Community of Women in High School Sports**, and she shared that her number one tool was to "Be Empathetic," even when you are having a tough day!

As a young AD, Jen mentioned that she felt she had to be "Tough" to be a leader, but she learned over time she could still be tough but at the same time, she could have true Empathy for the people whose lives you touch.

I really encourage all of you to check out Jen's website for the Global Community of Women in High School Sports – it's a great resource for any Athletic Director.

Our podcast guests were mostly high school Athletic Directors, but we also had 3 separate Student Athlete Panels. One of them had Samantha Migliore, a senior and a 3-sport athlete at Clay High

School in Green Cove Springs, Florida and she shared the importance of Athletic Directors having Empathy for their student athletes.

This is coming from the perspective of a very successful, high school student athlete, who also performs at the highest level in the classroom! Here is a "bonus" tool from me - It definitely pays off to listen to your student leaders!

Finally, Doug Stephens is a long-time coach and high school Athletic Director, who also has a great perspective from his many years as a top-rated high school basketball official. Doug is now the senior pastor at Fellowship Midway Church outside of Tallahassee, Florida. Doug shared the important tool of Loving and Encouraging the people you serve! He said, "The more you love and the more you encourage, the better off you're going to be!"

How cool is that? As you are putting your Toolbox together, make sure you try to have Compassion, Empathy, and Love as tools you can access in your Athletic Director Toolbox!

# CHAPTER 6

Tool #15 – Document Everything!

This Tool was mentioned by 8 of our Athletic Directors and it was expressed in a couple of different ways, including writing things down the old school way along with using computer documenting with files.

Dr. Chris Hobbs, CMAA and Athletic Director at The King's Academy in West Palm Beach, Florida suggested going old school and using "a Yellow Legal Pad and a pen and WRITE everything down!"

Chris went on to share that by doing this, he feels it actually "frees your mind up, and it acts as an External Brain, allowing you to Focus better!" Dr. Hobbs is quite the reader and researcher so take this tool suggestion to heart! This is something I already use when meeting with a coach or a parent.

Annette Scogin, CMAA and former NIAAA President started out by stressing that you "Need to know the legal ramifications of everything you do and of everyone around you." You especially need to know your District and County regulations and the NIAAA's Legal Courses are another great resource to develop this "tool" for your Toolbox!

Rocky Gillis, CAA (our very FIRST Podcast guest!) and the Athletic Director for the Broward County Athletic Association in Florida talked about helping a new AD to come up with a system that will help them "Document the Details" in everything that they do. Rocky feels this tool allows them to use all of the other tools that they will need to do the very best job that they can!

One of our International Athletic Directors, Catherine Tanco-Ong, CMAA and AD at the Brent International School in the Philippines. Coach Cat stressed the importance of Documenting "Everything" not just from a legal standpoint but also from an organizational perspective! Having it written down allows you to always look back and make sure you are doing what you "say" you are doing!

Jon Payne, CMAA from Ohio and a long-time teammate on the NIAAA Certification Committee suggested staying current on technology but continue to "backup" everything on paper. Jon likes Excel Spreadsheets for the accuracy they provide! I use them as well - I cannot tell you how many times I use a spreadsheet during the week but for me they are indispensable in my daily routine!

Anne Julian, CAA and Athletic Director at Holy Cross High School in Kentucky had an interesting take on this particular tool, saying, "Never handle a piece of paper more than twice – either file it, or throw it away." File (Document) the important pieces of paper! I like that phrase – never handle a piece of paper more than twice! What do you think?

Casey Thiele, CAA and the Escambia County (Florida) Athletic Director along with Darryl Nance, CMAA and the County Athletic Director for Greenville Co. Schools in Greenville, South Carolina each had a different take on "Documenting" as they both talked about the importance of using a "Journal" to help them record and to also review the events of the day or week.

Casey said that "If I write things down, it ingrains them and helps me organize my thoughts so I can do a better job!" Darryl said, "You have to Journal, and you have to Document." He feels that this allows you to "Know where you are, to know why you have done things, and to make sure you're staying true to who you are!"

Keeping a Journal is really a very cool idea – and another great tool – for your Athletic Director Toolbox!

For you stat geeks, here is a statistic … the Athletic Director Toolbox tools that we have shared so far, represent just 6% of the 475 suggestions that we received from our podcast guests, and while these are ALL Great Suggestions for Athletic Directors and Coaches – both New AD's and even Experienced AD's – we still have a lot more to share!

Next up, the **TOP 14** suggested tools in the Educational AD Podcast's Athletic Directors Toolbox!

# CHAPTER 7

Tool #14 – Be Flexible, Try New Things, & Keep an Open Mind

The ability to be Flexible is Tool # 14 and it was mentioned by 9 of our Athletic Directors. Also included in this Tool Category was Keeping an Open Mind, along with a willingness to Try New Things.

Kippie Crouch, CAA and Athletic Director from Out of Door Academy in Bradenton, Florida mentioned Flexibility as her #1 Toolbox Tool, stating she wishes (like most of us!) that she would have had a little more flexibility when she started out.

We've already heard from Chris Hall, CMAA from Discovery High School in Georgia and Dan Talbot, CMAA from Florida along with Charlie Marello, who is the Principal at Niceville (FL) High School who all had Flexibility as one of their three tools in their AD Toolbox.

Josh Blumenthal from St. Stephens Episcopal School in Austin, Texas says, "Flexibility is the Name of the Game" and how AD's need to also know the other schedules and events at their school – and be flexible when scheduling to build and maintain good relationships with the other departments.

Shay Steele from Walnut Hills High School in Ohio talked about the importance of "Keeping an Open Mind" and using life experiences along with your college and "book" experiences to allow you to see the value in something that you might not have ever thought of yourself! Another great idea and tool – Keep an Open Mind!

Shannon Klassen, who is the new Executive Director for the Canadian Interscholastic Athletic Administrators Association also felt that having an open mind was a key tool for Athletic Directors.

I really think this is so very important – just from a mental health and morale standpoint! Have you ever had a boss or supervisor that answered your suggestion with "We don't do it that way" or "That's not going to work!" Don't be a leader like that! Keep an Open Mind!

Jim Harris, CMAA and AD at T.C. Williams High School (Remember the Titans!) in Virginia came on very similar to Shannon stating, "The Worst Words in the English Language are – We've Always Done It This Way!" I'll say it again - Don't be that kind of leader! Keep an Open Mind!

# CHAPTER 8

Tool #13 – <u>Have a Sense of Humor & Stay Positive!</u>

The number of Athletic Directors suggesting tools in this category jumps up to 14 which is the largest increase we have seen.

Jessica Upchurch, CAA and the Director of Athletics at Sebastian River High School in Florida emphasized that we all have a very special job, a very cool job, and the essence of what we do starts with playing games and having fun! Remember to have FUN!

Pete Shambo, CMAA and recently retired Athletic Director at Penfield High School in New York, and my longtime "boss" on the NIAAA's Certification Committee, shared that we need to remember – even though we all really want to win – that It is only a game and that whether we win or lose, we are still dealing with kids (student athletes) and that we need to make it fun!" Thanks Pete! You always made it fun for us on Certification!

Rebeca Moe from University Prep in Seattle also stated the importance of having a sense of humor as we are dealing with kids most of our day. She said to remember that Coaches and Parents can occasionally act "like kids" so keep that Sense of Humor Tool handy in your toolbox!

Joey Struwe, CMAA and Athletic Director at Lincoln High School in South Dakota and another member of the NIAAA's Certification Committee talked about using humor in his daily routine.

Joey says, "Take the JOB seriously, but don't take yourself too seriously!" Joey succeeded me as Co-Vice Chair on Certification, and I can attest, he has THIS tool in his toolbox!

Becky Moran, CMAA and Director of Athletics at Round Lake High School in Illinois shared the importance of remembering to ENJOY what we get to do!

Becky shared, "If you're having a rough day, go out and watch a freshman team or a JV team practice to help recharge yourself!"

Becky is such a great leader for her school and the NIAAA and here she shares a really great idea!

Dr. Kaleb Stoppel, CMAA and the Director of Athletics at Olathe East H.S. in Kansas along with being an adjunct professor for the William Woods University Online Master's Degree in Athletic Administration stressed that "We have the Best Job in the World" and to remember that "We actually get paid to watch practices and game – what's more fun than that?"

I agree 100% as my "catch phrase" when someone asks me how my day is going, I replay that "I'm Living the Dream!" Make sure YOU are having fun!

Lyle Livengood, CAA and Athletic Director at West Port High School in Ocala, Florida stated the importance of remaining "Positive in the face of challenges."

Lyle feels you need to be a "Glass half FULL" kind of person and approach your day by "Trying to say Yes" will help take care of a lot of the challenges you face.

I told Lyle that I jokingly will say, "An Optimist can never be pleasantly surprised," but I also believe that he is right about being a Glass Half Full kind of AD! Stay Focused on the Positive!

Drew Hanson was a great podcast guest, and as a longtime coach, the former Executive Director of the CIAAA, the Canadian Interscholastic Athletic Administrators Association had an interesting take on this stating that "it can be a tough job, with highs and lows, but by keeping a really Positive Attitude, you'll be able to come through for your students and your coaches."

We also heard from the great Marc "Hutch" Hunter, CMAA and the Executive Director of the Utah Interscholastic Athletic Administrators Association who really emphasized the importance of remembering that "it's Interscholastic Athletics – it's about the kids!"

Hutch continued, saying "Not everyone will get to have a "Winning Season" or experience a "State Championship" season. He also stressed that "We are in the business of Educational Athletics – not college, and not the pros!" and "Let's make their (the kids) experience a great one – Win or Lose!"

Thanks Hutch! You really hit this on the head! And take a listen to his podcast, The UIAAA Connection, as he has some really cool guests on it!

Antony Fisher, CMAA and the Director of Athletics for the Minneapolis Public School System and the creator of NOMAD – the National Organization of Minority Athletic Directors - also stressed that "we need to create a Great Experience for the kids" and he outlined a 3-stage process to achieve this!

It was a great model for an Athletic Philosophy, an Athletic Department, or for a Team or Coach, as well as a great tool on its own!

Teresa Gunter is the AD at Leon High School in Tallahassee, Florida and she focused on the importance of an Athletic Director being more than positive – you should be EXCITED about your job! Teresa said "…if you're not excited about being an Athletic Director, something is wrong!" Be Excited Every Day! Not everyone gets to be an Athletic Director! Be EXCITED to be an Athletic Director!

Let's review - Tool # 13 included the following ideas:

Have a Sense of Humor, Have FUN, and Try to be … No, you NEED to be Positive. Oh yea - and Get Excited about being an Athletic Director!

# CHAPTER 9

Tool #12 – Integrity

This was a really interesting category to me. Remember, I took the tools that were suggested by our guests and then "Arranged" then into my own specific categories. For this particular category (tool), we had 19 Athletic Directors use words such as Integrity, Trust, Consistency, Authenticity, and Accountability, and I also included a couple of suggested "tools" that focused on the idea of Sportsmanship.

Leading off we have Tara Osbourne, CAA and Athletic Director at Prattville Christian Academy in Alabama who shared the importance of being "Open and Honest from the beginning," and she continued this theme stressing how important it is to "Be honest when you are getting to know your staff." Some wise words from one of our profession's best!

Two guests that we have already heard from also appear in this category. Dan Talbot, CMAA from Florida felt that "Trust" was possibly the most important tool for Athletic Directors by stating, "Your word should mean more than a signed contract!"

Texas Tech's Ashton Washington shared that Authenticity was something that Athletic Directors and Coaches needed in their toolbox as "Everything else you do as a leader will ring hollow if people think that you are not authentic!"

Andy Warner is a member of two different Athletic Hall of Fames in Florida and also happens to be the Director of Soccer at the Maclay School in Tallahassee, Florida where I was the Athletic Director.

Coach Warner said that "Values and Consistency were keys to his team's success," which includes multiple Florida State High School Titles over a 30+ year career.

Andy also said that it was important to "Have a clear idea of your values and have an idea of where you're going," and then the importance of "staying Consistent to those values regarding everything." Wise words from a Master Coach and Leader!

Kelly Fish, CMAA is the Athletic Director at Curry Ingram School in Nashville, Tennessee and she is also a member of the NIAAA's National Teaching Faculty.

When asked what tools she would put into a new Athletic Director's Toolbox, she spoke about the importance of being "Consistent, and always model what you expect."

Mark Greenburg was one of the members of our Texas High School Student Athlete Panel and he said AD's need to "hire good coaches, and then you need to Trust them!" Wise words coming from someone who is still competing for his school!

Of course, an AD is going to mentor and teach the coaches they hire, but you also have to have the tool of "Trust" in their toolbox so they can continue to grow!

Dr. Dustin Smith, CMAA – the Good Doctor – and the Director of Athletics at Greenwood Middle-High School in Greenwood, Arkansas also said that Integrity was a key tool for success, saying "You have to operate with Absolute Integrity from the get-go," and "there's never a wrong time to do the right thing... you've got to do what you say you're going to do!"

Marion House, CAA and Assistant Athletic Director at Nixa High School in Missouri shared that for her, Integrity is "... at the end of the day, you know that you've done the Best that you could to put the kids first, put safety first, and that you've helped them grow into the best person they could be." Wow - THAT is a great description of Integrity!

Rob Paschall, a longtime coaching friend and a very successful high school football coach in the state of Texas said that Integrity is "knowing what you will accept and what you will not accept," and then making sure you stay true to yourself.

Roger Mayo, CMAA and recently retired District Athletic Director for the Escambia County School District in Florida used the term "Silent Leadership" to help earn the Trust of the people (kids, coaches, parents) that Athletic Directors work with.

Roger also mentioned how important it was to "don't be a hypocrite" by asking your coaches to work on Professional

Development and then you, as an AD, not do the same.

FYI - Roger was the FIAAA President just prior to my term and I can attest that he had the Trust of our entire FIAAA Board of Directors! Also - Silent Leadership ... I like that term!

Jamie Sheetz, CMAA out of Park City, Utah stated that "The number one thing we have to build with our coaches is Trust," and "Trust is the currency that we have with Coaches, with Student Athletes, and with Staff ... without it you won't be able to go anywhere."

Don Baker, CAA one of the great hosts of the Hangin' with the AD Podcast talked about the importance of Sportsmanship which, in my opinion, really embodies all these qualities (tools) that have been mentioned such as Integrity, Consistency, Trust, and Accountability.

Dr. Keisha Knowles, CAA who is the Athletic Director and the Athletic Trainer (!) at Rockdale, County Schools in Georgia mentioned that part of the Integrity component is that Athletic Directors need to remember, "There are NO Minor Sports!"
She followed this up by stating, "to at least one kid on that team, THAT sport is the most important sport, and those athletes need to know that it is important to you as well!"

Josh Scott, CMAA is the Springfield, Missouri District Athletic Director, along with being the long time NIAAA Secretary. Josh has two lists for all the sports his schools offer. One of the lists says, "Educational Based Sports" and the other list says, "Major Sports."
The first list has EVERY SPORT that is offered in the district, but the second list is EMPTY!
This is to show that Josh feels whatever sport a kid is participating in; it IS a Major Sport to that kid! I think this illustrates the "Integrity Tool" pretty good!

Darlene Bible, CMAA and the Athletic Director at Harvard-Westlake School in California shared that as leaders, Athletic Directors need to always be "Accountable." She stated, "As the

Athletic Director, you OWN the department, and any failure is your failure." Some very strong words, but I think that they ring true! As Leaders, we must be accountable!

To review – this tool included Integrity, Trust, Consistency, Authenticity, and Accountability, along with the goal of teaching Sportsmanship. Make sure you have room in your Toolbox for these very important tools!

Next up – Tool # 11 in the Athletic Director's Toolbox as shared by the Athletic Director interviews from the Educational AD Podcast!

# CHAPTER 10

Tool #11 – <u>Patience!</u>

For our next Tool, 19 of our Athletic Directors mentioned "Patience," along with the importance of "Having a Thick Skin" and the ability to be a "Diplomat."

Kiesha Brown, CMAA and she is the K-8 Athletic Director at The Galloway School in Atlanta, Georgia. Kiesha mentioned "Patience" as one of her Top Tools when working with student athletes, particularly at the middle school level! She also shared that this comes in handy in her "other job" as a high school and college Basketball Official! As an official myself, I strongly concur!

Dixie Westcott, CMAA and Program Director for the William Woods University (Missouri) online Master's in Athletic Administration shared that, "You have to be patient and not expect to resolve everything at once!" She actually said it again, "Be Patient!"

Anne Campbell, CMAA and Director of Athletics for the Grand Rapids School District in Minnesota shared that you need to "Give yourself time to learn," You're not going to "get it" all at once! "Be patient and give yourself time!"

Rob Seymour, CMAA and Athletic Director at Fishers High School in Indiana also had "Patience" in his Toolbox, using an acronym PQR where Patience was one of Rob's 3 P-words! Listen to his episode or check it out on YouTube to get all 9 PQR "tools" as they are great ones!

David Marlow, CMAA and the AD at Mount Mansfield Union High School in Jericho, Vermont, had Patience in his toolbox saying, "Patience is involved with every decision you make as an Athletic Director."

Michelle Noeth, CAA and Director of Athletics at Los Altos High School in Los Altos, California said that "You can't worry about your mistakes!" She also shared that "Life has Speed-bumps but you're going to be ok!" Some really good advice from one of our up-and-coming Athletic Directors!

Mark Rosenbalm, CMAA is a member of our FIAAA Board of Directors and he's also the County Athletic Director for Collier County in SW Florida. Mark shared that you need to "Limit your time with Grumblers and the Complainers," and "95% of your people are going to be on your side so don't let the 5% bring you down!"

"Having a Thick Skin" was shared by Dr. Danielle LaPoint of Manatee County in Florida. She said, "You're not always going to make everyone happy – you have to do what's best for your school and your teams."

This is a huge "tool" to have as there will be times when a parent, fan, coach, or community member does not like your decision. As Dr. LaPointe said, "do what's best for your school, and have a thick skin!"

Nathan Stanley, CAA and Director of Athletics for Lake Oswego High School just outside of Portland, Oregon also felt that "Having a Thick Skin" was a key tool to have. Nathan said we need to be "Anti-Fragile" which means when someone criticizes us, we need to use that to be Stronger which is the opposite if being Fragile – BE Anti-Fragile!

Great stuff from my Boxer Brother as we are both proud alums of Pacific University in Forest Grove, Oregon.

Ann Stewert, CAA and Athletic Director at Los Alamos High School in New Mexico also thought that "Having a Thick Skin" was a valuable tool. I think Ann's experience in Law Enforcement probably helped her with this tool!

Ann also acknowledged that this can be hard to do but she also stressed that frequently "a negative comment is not about you personally but about the situation." Ann also shared that since becoming a parent herself that she has been able to see the "other side" better which has helped! It's always great to visit with Ann Stewert!

My good friend and old high school teammate, Robert Blackman, CAA and Athletic Director at R.A. Long High School in Longview, Washington had a slightly different take on this tool by saying "You can't take everything personally!"

Robert very accurately stated that most of us that go into athletics and athletic administration do so because "We love it," and when we get criticized, it can hurt! Robert's advice is spot on, "Don't take it personally..." and he also says that this is "Easy to say but sometimes hard to do!" Having said that, try and remember to NOT take those critical comments personally!

Carol Dozibrin, CMAA a long-time Athletic Director and Coach who is now the Executive Director for the New Hampshire Athletic Directors Association felt that "Knowing and Understanding the Culture of your school was key," and that this "takes time to do."

Carol is really one of our professions best and she and I are part of the team creating a new LTI course! It's great to be able to work with someone as sharp as Carol!

My FIAAA mentor, the great Dan Comeau, CMAA and Director of Mentoring for the FIAAA is next to weigh in on this tool and Dan had a similar take to Carol's on this saying that an Athletic Director needs to take the time – be patient - and "Get to know your student athletes."

Catherine Tanco-Org, CMAA from the Brent International School in the Philippines said that being able to be a "Diplomat" was an important tool.  Obviously "Patience" is certainly a very important tool in the toolbox of any Diplomat! Is it in yours?

Anne Julian, CAA and Athletic Director at Holy Cross High School in Kentucky had one of the most interesting responses for this category, sharing a book that she had read called, Happy Kids Don't Punch You in the Face! It's a real book - Look it up!

Brad Montgomery, CAA and Athletic Director at Seabreeze High School in Ormond Beach, Florida offered the tool of "You need to be willing to work with everyone."

This means working with "Administration, Staff, and everyone all the way down to the kids!" Brad works at a large public school, and he does a great job with this Athletic Director tool!

Also mentioning Patience as one of their Tools are previous contributors Pete Shambo, CMAA from Penfield High School in New York, and Charlie Marello, Principal at Niceville High School in Florida. We also heard from Teresa Gunter, the Athletic Director at Leon High School in Tallahassee, Florida who shared the phrase, "You gotta have Teflon Skin!"

Well, that wraps up the first half of our Toolbox Top Twenty! Let's review them –

#20    1 time - Unique Tools: Tape Measure, Whistle, +Turds

#19    2 times – Budget, Spouse, and Branding!

#18    3 times - Know your School District Policy Manual

#17    4 times – Have a Social Media Presence

#16    5 times – Have Empathy & Compassion

#15    8 times – Document Everything.

#14    9 times – Be Flexible & Open to New Things

#13    14 times – Laugh & Have a Sense of Humor

#12    18 times – Trust, Authenticity, and Consistency

#11    19 times – Patience, along with Have a Thick Skin

For all of you Stat Geeks - ALL of these tool suggestions add up to 89 tools or a little over **18% of the total** suggestions we received during the interviews. Are they all important tools for an Athletic Director? <u>You bet they are</u>, but we have a LOT more to share!

We have gone over the first half of the Educational AD Podcast's Toolbox Top Twenty – now let's find out the Top TEN Toolbox Tools as suggested by the podcast guests.

# CHAPTER 11

Tool #10 – Listen!

As we move into the TOP TEN Tools, 20 of our Athletic Directors mentioned the ability to "Listen" as one of their most important tools! Oh, how true is that! Also included in this category were some related ideas such as being able to say, "I don't know, but I'll find out" along with the awareness of sitting down and having those "Hard Conversations."

Allison Fondale, CMAA and Athletic Director at St. Mary's High School in Maryland mentioned Listening as a key tool. She said you need to "Listen to your student athletes and listen to your coaches," and when appropriate, "Take their advice."

Allison started her very successful student athlete leadership program after listening to the suggestions from some of her school's student leaders! Listen!

Stephanie Blackwell, CMAA and Athletic Director at Oklahoma's Bixby High School (and a member of the NIAAA's Certification Committee) mentioned that it is, "OK to not know the answer," if a parent asks a question, but tell them "I will find out and get back to you!"

Stephanie felt this was a key leadership tool as it allowed her to be Transparent while also allowing her to not be put on the spot!

Dr. Lisa Langston, CMAA and Ft. Worth, Texas Athletic Director – along with being the current NIAAA President - said "Learn to Listen, and as you listen, if it's a parent that's complaining about something, listen for where there might be elements of truth!"

This is such a key element of success for any Athletic Director – I know it was for me when I finally learned to use the tool of Listening!

Deb Savino, CMAA and Assistant Athletic Director at Ransom Everglades School in South Florida also stressed "listening" as one of her important tools saying. "Always listen to what they have to say and, when they are done – ask them, Is there anything else?"

Deb feels this helps show that you are really listening to them which is really what most parent conversations are about – they simply want to be heard! Great advice!

Rich Barton, CMAA and Director of Athletics and Assistant Principal at Richfield High School in Utah, along with being an NIAAA Past President felt that Listening was one of his most important tools – so important that he features it prominently in two recent NIAAA Leadership Training courses that he has helped author which are LTI 706 - Coaching the Coaches and the new course, LTI 719 - Partnering with Parents which I get to be a part of!

Rich summed things up with this statement, "Listeners are Learners, and Learners are Listeners!" Make sure you have Listening as a tool in your Athletic Director Toolbox

Dan Schuster, CMAA and Director of Learning for the NFHS, the National Federation of High Schools shared that listening to "Your staff, your coaches, and your colleagues" was "critically important" so you can "Understand where they are coming from and how they are feeling so you can relate to and take care of them!" Take care of the people you care about! Listen to them!

Stacey Segal, CMAA and Assistant Director of Athletics for the Dallas Independent School District said that listening was one of her top tools especially to "help you communicate with all of the stakeholders including parents, coaches, media members and the board…"

One of Stacey's other tools was "Communication" and she tied it in with Listening. Hopefully, you have seen the value that our Athletic Directors have placed on Listening – make sure this "tool" is in your Toolbox!

Tim Leeseburg, CAA and Athletic Director at Plant City High School East of Tampa, Florida said that you need to "Listen to your coaches … listen to your administrators … and most importantly, listen to your parents…"

Tim added that "often you want to interrupt and address a point (I know that was always a struggle for me!) but just try to really LISTEN to them!" Some wise words from a great Athletic Director!

Gary Stevens, CMAA and Director of Athletics at Maine's prestigious Thornton Academy and a long-time member of the NIAAA Publications Committee, said that "The number one tool you need is the ability to Listen!"

Gary talked about the need to "Learn the Culture of your school," and you need to listen to everyone to learn that culture!" Gary continued, "Even for an experienced AD, you need to learn the culture!" Great advice from a true Master Athletic Administrator!

Teg Cosgriff, CMAA and Athletic Director for the Westbrook Public School District in Westbrook, Connecticut shared that "People want to be heard and they need to be heard," and by listening, this "helps you formulate and make decisions … and those decisions will be informed ones."

Teg also added that most of the time, "people just want to be heard," which is so true! Learn to Listen!

Ken Edwards, CMAA and the Director of Athletics at Jamestown High School in Virginia talked about listening this way – Ken feels that you need to learn how to have those "Hard conversations with Parents, Coaches, and others…" and that during those conversations "Make sure you listen to what they're telling you … be transparent!"

Ken talked about some of the hard conversations he has had to have this year with Covid issues along with eligibility issues. As Ken said, don't be afraid to "Walk into those Hard Conversations."

Dr. Greg Dale, the Director of Sport Psychology at Duke University said he was going to, "Put on a big pair of EARS so you can Listen…" Dr. Dale spoke about the "Change" that occurs when you go from being an Assistant Coach to now being a Head Coach, or when a Head Coach becomes the Athletic Director.

Greg also used the visual of, "the new head coach has only moved 12 inches down the bench from where they used to sit, but its and entirely new View … and the best thing they can do, is Listen!" The same is true when you become an Athletic Director – make sure you have that "big pair of Ears" in your Athletic Director Toolbox!

We also heard from several previous contributors to the Toolbox Top Twenty who listed "Listening" as one of their tools including Ann Stewert CAA and Roger Mayo CMAA, along with Hall of Fame Soccer Coach Andy Warner, and University Prep (WA) Athletic Director Rebecca Moe.

Your humble author also put down "Listening" as one of my top tools! Oh, how I wish that I could have had this tool in my toolbox earlier in my career! And I speak from the position of having to have learned this the hard way – please make sure that the ability to LISTEN is one of the tools in your Athletic Director Toolbox!

# CHAPTER 12

Tool # 9 – <u>Vision, Values, Perspective, and Alignment</u>

This was another eclectic category as I tried to link the common theme to a variety of toolbox answers. For this particular tool category, we had a total of 23 Athletic Directors who contributed, but I really feel their answers are all Philosophically "Aligned." Having your own vision and making sure your vision was aligned with the School District was shared multiple times. Also, knowing your own "Core Values" along with knowing your "WHY" were tools that ended up in this category.

Ernest Robertson, Jr. CMAA and longtime Athletic Director at Palmer Trinity School in South Florida – also my tag team partner a couple of times for an NIAAA parenting workshop – stressed the importance of "Having the Support of the Board" as a tool.

Ernest said, "Make sure you have the full support of the Leadership at the school," and "Make sure your values align with the values of the school!"

If you come in with a philosophy of Educational Based Athletics, and the school has the philosophy of "we just want to win," there will probably be some challenges! Make sure you have the support of the school's leadership!

Mark Lee, CAA and the Athletic Director at Hernando High School in Florida shared that you need to, "Have a Plan ... something that you want to put your name on and that will put your school in the best position for success!'

Mark also referred to "the Dash," meaning the "time between when you started at the school, and when you finally leave ... have a plan so your Dash will be clear to you and to everyone else!"

Staying in Florida we also heard from Pam Cawley, CAA and the Director of Athletics at Foundation Christian Academy in Valrico, Florida. Pam also felt that "Having the support of your Administration," was key as she added, "You're doing so many things including pulling kids out of classes to go to games and spending more money than they might want..." so knowing you have that support allows you to do your job to the best of your ability. Administrative Support is Key to any Athletic Director's Success!

Kristin Peeples, CAA and Director of Athletics at Nature Coast Technical High School in Brooksville, Florida really emphasized "Staying Positive, and always remember your WHY."

Kristin said, "… this job can sometimes be draining, but if you can always remember your Why, I think it brings out the best in you as an individual, and it also allows those around you to see that everything is going to be ok!" I've gotten to know Kristin from our state association's Representative Assembly, and I can attest that she definitely Knows her Why! Great Stuff!

Quante Speight, CAA and Athletic Director at Mallard Creek High School in North Carolina put a different "tool" into this category by suggesting that a Job Description be present.

Quante also said, "Understanding that the role of an Athletic Director is a lifestyle unlike no other," and that he has even "Created his own job description at some of the districts I have worked in…" just as a reminder of what the job entails.

If your school or district does not have an official job description for your position, you should sit down with your supervisor and start the process to create one! THIS is a very important tool for the toolbox!

One of our "Celebrity" podcast guests was the great Jay Hammes, CMAA and the Director of the SAFESPORTZONE program that is used by schools from across the country.

Jay is also a longtime Athletic Director who really knows his stuff and he shared the importance of "Building relationships with and working with your school board" to ensure your policies are aligned.

Jay also spoke about the process of creating an "Athletic Board," including parents along with staff members to "Come up with improvement ideas and suggestions" and then working with your district's "Emergency Response Team" to ultimately take these ideas to the school board for final approval.

We also heard from Brian Nolan, CAA and the Athletic Director at Charlotte High School in Punta Gorda, Florida. Brian shared a very practical tool that I chose to include in this category which was

"Know your Facility" including "know how to shut off the sprinklers when they come on during a game ... know how to turn on the scoreboard ... know how to get ahold of the officials ..."

This tool could have been placed in a couple of spots, but I felt it belonged here as it was a good application of having VISION! The vision of Knowing your Facility! Thanks for sharing this, Brian!

Next, we have Shea Collins, CAA and Director of Activities and Athletics at Midlothian High School in Virginia. Shea offered a great tool to "Measure Success," as she offered up a "Ruler" as part of her idea of "watch your program and see where you're at and where you're going ..."

Shea also reminded us that, "Success isn't going to happen overnight," but she also recommended to "Put some marks on that ruler to see how far you've come." Some great advice and a great "tool" for your toolbox!

Laura Zamora was one of the youngest contributors to our list of Toolbox tools, but she spoke with wisdom beyond her years! Laura actually used to be a coach at one my schools, and while she did a fantastic job, she is now the senior Manager at City Year in Miami, Florida, an organization that develops coaches to go out and support the growth of students in under-resourced schools, while then cultivating their skills to be leaders in their communities and careers.

Laura uses her experiences as a successful Athlete and as a Coach to help her team create the next generation of Leaders! One of Laura's tools was "Having a Vision ..." and "knowing what Success looks like to you, for the student-athletes, and for the coaches." Definitely a great tool!

Cassidy Lichtman, a two-time NCAA All-American at Stanford, was a very cool person to interview as she shared her experiences playing for the USA National Volleyball Team and also as a Professional Player overseas. Cassidy is now the director of P/ATH which is a non-profit organization which works within the sports world to better develop skills around empathy and empowerment for athletes.

Cassidy feels that you must "Have a Reason for What you do," whether you are coaching kids or coaching coaches! Cassidy shared that she has played for the "very best" coaches in the volleyball world and they all had a "Reason" for what they did! Another great tool for the toolbox!

We also heard from the following Athletic Directors who have already appeared in the Toolbox Top Twenty:

Andy Warner - Florida (Have Vision)

Carol Dozibrin – New Hampshire (Aligned with your Board)

Nathan Stanley – Oregon (Keep a Big Perspective)

Rob Pashcall – Texas (Be able to hire your staff)

Drew Hanson – Canada (Know – write down - your Philosophy)

Rob Seymour – Indiana (Perspective)

John Drake – North Carolina (Know the Culture)

Michelle Noeth – California (Have a Job Description)

Antony Fisher – Minnesota (Perspective)


Thanks to all of these great contributors for helping to stock our Athletic Director's Toolbox!

Now, let's move on to Tool # 8

# CHAPTER 13

## Tool # 8 – Hire Great People & Support Your Staff

Tool #8 was suggested by a total of 28 of our podcast guests and it was expressed in a variety of ways. Some said, "Hire great people" while others mentioned taking care of the "Custodians, Administrative Assistants, and Facilities Crew."

A few also mentioned the importance of "Delegating" responsibilities to these great people and one expressed this by saying, "Protect Your Principal" which is a VERY important tool!

Let's look at these tools as they were shared by our panel of Athletic Directors.

First off, we get to hear from my very good friend and NIAAA Certification Committee "Brother" Tol Gropp, who is a CMAA and he's also the Athletic Director at Timberline High School in Boise, Idaho.

Tol is a big believer in "Delegating" responsibilities as not everyone has a dedicated Administrative Assistant or an Assistant Athletic Director, but "we all have coaches who want to take on some administrative duties, "Which can lighten your load as the Athletic Director which will allow you to "do a better job" at what you're doing! Delegate! What a great idea!

Shelton Crews, a long-time friend – we met about 20 years ago while serving on the FHSAA Football Coaches Advisory Committee – who is now the Executive Director of the FACA (Florida Athletic Coaches Association) shared that, "The minute you walk on campus, there are two people you need to take care of … the Head Custodian and the Head Administrative Assistant, because they can make or break you!"

Shelton also shared that incredible value that is found in handing out "T-shirts, hats, and polos" to these groups (and others!) in your role as Athletic Director! This is another "tool" that I have used very successfully over the years, and I hope you will too!

Jay Radar, CAA is another veteran Florida Athletic Director from Palm Beach County who is retired but remains active as a substitute teacher and a state caliber Softball Umpire. Jay is also on our FIAAA

Board of Directors helping with the content of our online newsletter.

Jay's tool recommendations included making sure that you have developed "a great relationship with the head custodian and the administrative assistant."

He also said it helps to demonstrate some kind of awareness of the "Academic World" to develop a relationship with the faculty! Jay was also an English teacher prior to becoming an Athletic Director so you can see where he is coming from! Some more great advice!

Peggy Seegers-Braun, CMAA is the Athletic Director at Divine Savior Holy Angels High School in Milwaukie, Wisconsin. Peggy's toolbox includes the tool of "Surrounding yourself with Great people!"

Peggy feels that "When you hire people that are better than you, then YOU will rise to that level!" Another Master Athletic Administrator that wants you to have the Tool of being in the presence of great people! Make sure you have this tool in your Athletic Director Toolbox!

Marcus Gabriel, CAA and Director of Athletics at American High School in Hialeah, Florida. Marcus is also the 2021-22 FIAAA President Elect, and he strongly suggests that you "Need to surround yourself with very POSITIVE People."

He went on to say that "When you're starting out…you need to stay away from the Nay Sayers and those with Negative Energy …" Another great tool to have – find Positive People and surround yourself with them!

Nicole Ebsen, CAA and Athletic Director at Morton High School in Berwyn, Illinois. An interesting note, Nicole's school holds the Illinois High School Association "record" for the most Fan Busses!

When she was on the podcast, Nicole's toolbox suggestions included "Finding that TEAM of people that will do anything for you, and then take care of those people!" She mentioned it could be the "maintenance staff, clerical staff, assistant coaches, or sport coordinators…" but to make sure "You take care of those people who take care of You!"

One of the great joys of our profession is working with our own

"Team" to make sure our events come off smoothly! THAT is a valuable tool!

Mike McGurk, CMAA and Athletic Director at Lee's Summit High School and also the 2021 NIAAA President Elect! Mike shared that one of his most important tools was "the ability to VALUE everyone."

Mike went on to say, "that might be the number one tool ... the ability value the custodian, to value your secretary, your coaches..." Mike felt this was critical not just for a new Athletic Director but for all AD's.

Josh Matthews, CMAA and Athletic Director at Pope High School in Georgia and one of the hosts of the very successful podcast, Hangin' with the AD! Josh shared that this was one of the toughest questions to limit it to just three, but he did share the importance of having an Administrative Assistant who speaks the language of Athletics.

Even if you cannot find a fulltime salaried position, try to find a parent (or coach) to help take some of the load off of your plate. Just another example of finding and valuing the people who help make our profession so great!

Don Baker, CAA and Director of Athletics for the Cobb County School District in Georgia and the other host of the Hangin' with the AD Podcast used the very cool term of "Shield of Immunity" referring to the idea that "I will always fight for you and protect and support you, as long as you don't fall outside of the Shield of Immunity!"

Don felt that by creating this feeling of support within your department that the coaches "will feed off of you and work for you!" I really like that – The Shield of Immunity!

Deb Margolis is the Athletic Director at TERRA - The Environmental Research Institute in South Florida. Deb is a long time Florida Athletic Director who built Coral Reef High School into a powerhouse before moving on to lead the TERRA athletic program.

Deb shared "Surround yourself with a great team," and went on to say that her team was Everybody including, "... the security officer, the teachers, custodians, athletic trainer and the coaches …"

She added that, "… everybody needs to know that you value what they do," along with, "You can't do your job without their help!" Create a "Team" and then "Value" everyone's contribution – sounds like a great tool to me!

Lacey London, CAA is the Director of Athletics at Holy Names Academy in Seattle, Washington and she mentioned the importance of "taking care of your staff," including the "Secretary, the Custodian, the kitchen staff, the ticket takers, and the facilities crew."

Lacey also said you need to, "Get to know them beyond their jobs." She shared another good tip that she tries to, "Hand out extra swag," along with "… every year I make cookies for the support staff," and now they will make sure to ask, "Are you making the cookies this year?" Take Care of your "Team" is another great tool!

Kari Avila, CAA is someone I first met through the NIAAA Portal, and she is the Athletic Director at Salome High School in Arizona. Kari feels that you must "Support your coaches in their endeavors and their growth as leaders."

Kari stated that she was pushed and encouraged to grow in her position and that she wants to "Encourage my coaches to grow and get better." We all need some encouragement sometimes, and Kari gives us a great tool as a reminder to Support your Coaches!

Kelly Blount, CAA and Director of Athletics at Atlantic Coast High School in Jacksonville, Florida. Kelly is also on our FIAAA Board of Directors, and he and I spent a few years together serving on the FHSAA's Section I Appeals Board.

Kelly was slightly more specific with his support tool saying that "… the one thing I've found that was vital to my survival is to protect my principal!' He went on to say, "when you do that, you're going to have a good relationship with them and in turn, support from them."

As you work to support your staff, remember to support your principal by keeping them informed and by keeping them from being surprised! THIS is really an important tool to have in your Athletic Director Toolbox!

For this Tool, we also heard from these Athletic Directors who have already shared at least one time with another toolbox tool -

Ernest Robertson, CMAA – Florida (Support your Support Staff)

Joey Struwe, CMAA – South Dakota (Hire Great People)

Stacey Segal, CMAA – Texas (Hire Great People)

Pam Cawley, CAA – Florida (Hire Great People)

Marion House, CAA – Missouri (Delegate)

Dr. David Kelly, CAA – Ohio (Delegate)

Rob Pashcall – Texas (Hire Great People)

Quante Speight, CAA – North Carolina (Hire Great People)

Darlene Bible, CMAA – California (Hire Great People)

Bob Bruglio – Florida (Have a great Athletic Secretary)

Ben Center – Texas Student Athlete Panel (Hire Good Coaches)

Mark Rosenbalm, CMAA – Florida (Hire Great Coaches)

John Drake – North Carolina (Hire Great People)

Gary Stevens, CMAA – Maine (Hire a Great Athletic Trainer)

Brian Nolan, CAA – Florida (Take Care of the Custodians)

That is quite a collection of talent, all of whom felt that Hiring Great People and then Taking Care of Them was an important Tool to have in your Athletic Director Toolbox!

Now we move on to Tool # 7

# CHAPTER 14

Tool # 7 – Be Present in The Job

This tool was suggested by a total of 35 of our podcast guests and it was expressed in a variety of ways including Be Visible, Show Your Work Ethic, You have to have GRIT, Bring Passion, Roll up your sleeves, Learn the JOB! Get your Hands Dirty, and to Be Intentional!

Let's see which Athletic Directors put this Tool into their Toolbox!

Wayne Stofsky, the outstanding Athletic Director for the David Posnack School in Davie, Florida starts us off with the suggestion to "Be Seen" in your role as an Athletic Director. Athletics can and should be the "Face" of the school.

Wayne says you need to "Get to as many games and practices as you can," and he also shared the oft quoted lines, "Your Coaches and kids Don't care how much you know until they know how much you care and being SEEN helps show them that you care!" Wayne is spot on – get out there and Be Seen!

Steve McHale, CAA and Director of Athletics at Dr. Phillips High School in Orlando, Florida mentioned "Don't be afraid to get your hands dirty" as part of your role as a Leader.

Steve added, "Don't be afraid to pick up trash, or pick up a paint brush…" as it's "inspirational for the people on your team to see you doing what might be considered non-traditional jobs."

This is so true! When you can, get out of the office and see what else you can do to Get Your Hands Dirty!

Scott Drabczyk CAA and a Past President of the FIAAA along with being the current hair for the NIAAA's Hall of Fame Committee also weighed in on this tool!

Scott is also the Athletic Director at the brand-new Horizon High School in Orlando, Florida and Scott kept the theme of "clean" going by saying, "There is no task to big or small for an athletic director," including things like "Taking out the garbage, painting a field, or sweeping the floor before a game…" Scott stressed that these Dirty Details are what many people notice, and they can pay off in a big way!

Mike Ellson, CMAA from Nashville, Tennessee where is he the Athletic Director at Christ Presbyterian Academy showed up with this Tool. Mike has quite an impressive background as his school is one of the truly "Elite" school programs to have earned the NIAAA's Quality Program Award!

Mike shared the importance of having a strong "Work Ethic" in your toolbox. Mike said you "Should never let anyone outwork you," and added a point from the great coach, John Wooden and his Pyramid of Success, saying, "two of the foundation blocks of the Pyramid are Industriousness and Enthusiasm which means you should Work Hard, but also Have Fun!"

Mike topped it off by saying, "If you're having fun, that is a great way to Bless other people!" Mike Ellson, thanks for blessing us with this great tool!

Steve Throne, CMAA and Athletic Director from Millard South High School in Omaha, Nebraska and he was one of the very first "Outside of Florida Athletic Directors to reach out to the Educational AD Podcast and introduce himself! After spending a few minutes with him, I knew we had to get him on the show!

Steve shared his tool suggestion of "Don't be afraid to roll up your sleeves and go to work!" Another gem he shared was, "As an Athletic Director, you're never going to punch a time-clock" which we all know to be true!

Amber O'Malley, CAA also shared this tool. Amber is the Assistant Athletic Director at The Community School of Naples, in Southwest Florida along with being a member of our FIAAA Board of Directors.

Amber encourages Athletic Directors to embrace the practice of "Wearing Multiple Hats" stating, "you may get asked to run the scoreboard, or the videoboard" and that by taking on these new things, "You can find out that you're really good at something that you never thought you might do!"

Amber's role with FIAAA has her in charge of Special Events and every year at our state conference, she is embracing new things! Make sure you have "Multiple Hats" in your toolbox!

Jason Frey, CAA is another one of our great Florida and FIAAA Athletic Directors. Jason is the Director of Athletics at Pompano Beach Highs School in Pompano Beach, Florida. Jason works with Amber O'Malley on our Special Events Committee focusing on Hospitality, and he offers his take on this tool by sharing the importance of bringing "Passion" to the job.

Jason says, "If you don't have the passion for it, you're not going to be able to do this job!" Jason also said, "Athletic Directors are going 24-7 for 365 days a year!" and he added, "I think AD's might even go 367 days because of all the late night on the job as well as the afterhours texting that goes with it!"

I've seen Jason in action, and he certainly brings the Passion! Do you have Passion in your Toolbox?

Julie Renner, CAA and the Assistant Executive Director of the Ohio Interscholastic Athletic Administrators Association was a guest on the Educational AD Podcast just before accepting this new position.

As a long-time Athletic Director with a history of success she is highly qualified to weigh in on this and her contribution to this tool is really cool! Julie says, "You need to make a DEPOSIT into the lives of the people you serve."

Julie shares that you should never feel too important to those "jobs" that make up game days such as "Sweeping the floor, painting the lines, and picking up the trash." When you "make those deposits, those people become your biggest supporters and that makes your program stronger!"

Another great take on a very important tool – Make those Deposits into your program – and make sure this tool is in your toolbox!

Greg Warren is a CMAA, and he is the Director of Athletics for the New Paltz Central School District in New Paltz, New York. Greg and I first met as members of the first NIAAA Cohort Program and I immediately found him to be a real "Pro" as far as Educational Athletics is concerned!

Greg's contribution to the Toolbox includes the idea of "Know your Job and Learn your Job!" Greg stressed that our role as an Athletic Director is "Not a Fly-by-Night kind of job!" and that you should focus on "Learning how to do your current job to the very best of your ability, as opposed to the quickest way to learn it." Thanks for sharing this, Greg!

Susan Noonan is the Athletic Director at The Ursuline School in Dallas, Texas and in her podcast interview, she shared the tool of "Being Present ... 100% Be Present!" Susan also said, "The only way you can get to know your coaches and your players, and your parents is to be Present!"

Susan leads a fairly large department, but she also does a great job with all the programs she serves by Being Present." Make sure you are Present in your role as Athletic Director and make sure you have THIS tool in your Athletic Director Toolbox!

Nate Larsen, CMAA and Assistant Principal and Athletic Director at Logan View Jr/Sr. HS in Hooper, Nebraska also contributed this tool saying, "First and foremost, you have to have a Work Ethic," along with "You've got to be willing to jump in whatever the reason ..."

There are so many things that go into making an athletic event come off without a hitch but often there are "hitches" that go un-noticed because the Athletic Director stepped in and took care of it! Nate also included as part of the AD's Work Ethic to be "Intentional about getting to know the kids" as sometimes that does not occur naturally when you are no longer coaching a team.

It's great to see so many Athletic Directors place an importance on this tool – is Work Ethic in your toolbox?

Suzanne Vick is a great example of an "Unintended Consequence of the Pandemic" and what I mean by that is, I got to "meet" Suzanne at the 2020 NIAAA Virtual Conference and we have since become great friends and colleagues!

After appearing on the podcast, Suzanne shared her CMAA project idea with me and I gave her a couple of suggestions before she presented it! Of course, it was already a great project, but I got to learn a few new ideas from her, and she has since created some cool programs for her school - Curtis High School in University Place, Washington - along with collaborating with some other AD's in her area to overcome some Covid related challenges!

Suzanne shares her tool suggestion in this category by sharing a phrase that resonated with my former coaching life by stating, "You need to be an Athlete…" Suzanne elaborated on this by sharing "It's going to be hard; you're going to have to persevere…" and she finished by saying, "Go out and be loud in your space…" meaning find a way to encourage your kids, your coaches, and your stakeholders!"

I used to tell our football players, "Go out and be an athlete" as one of our "Hustle" catch phrases, so it immediately caught my ear. Make sure you have the "Be an Athlete Tool" in your Toolbox!

Jerri Kelly, CAA and Athletic Director at the very successful Lake Brantley High School in Altamonte Springs, Florida checks in with this tool category. Jerri was a partial inspiration for this book as each year at our FIAAA Conference, she facilitates a workshop called "The New AD's Toolbox" for our first-time attendees. I always loved that title and obviously borrowed it for the Toolbox Segment that we end each interview with!

Jerri's tool for this category is Be Present, but she describes it in a very specific way by stating, "Be present in your conversations with people!" She continued, "Take notes, and find out what matters to them, whether it's a coach, an athlete, or a parent."

Jerri also challenged us to "don't text or try to answer an email during a conversation! Be Present!" Another great tool suggestion and a different – more focused – way to be present!

Emily Barkley, CMAA and Athletic Director at Union Public Schools in Tulsa, Oklahoma is another new colleague I met during the 2020 NIAAA Virtual Conference. Emily does a great job for her teams, and she weighs in on this category with the importance of being "Visible" which she feels allows you to "Build relationships (see Tool #6) and trust (see Tool #9) by being seen by your coaches, your students, and your parents."

Emily told the story of as an 8th grade student-athlete, she was warming up for a basketball game and she saw her Athletic Director in the stands! She thought, "Oh my gosh, the Athletic Director is coming to a girls' basketball game!" Emily went on to share how that made a huge impression upon her and how "that was one of the things that drew me into this Profession!"

We always hear about how the kids are always watching us, and they are! Make sure you are Visible at your school – for the kids, for the coaches, and for the parents! Make sure this tool is in your Athletic Director Toolbox!

Previous contributors to the Toolbox Top Twenty who also mentioned THIS tool included –

Kippie Crouch, CAA – Florida (Passion)

Ashton Washington – Texas (Effort!)

Mark Lee, CAA – Florida (Be Involved)

Rich Barton, CMAA – Utah (Lift and Assist)

Kristin Peeples, CAA – Florida (Be Present)

Dr. Dustin Smith, CMAA – Arkansas (Intensity)

Deb Savino, CMAA – Florida (Control What You Can)

Jamie Sheetz, CMAA – Utah (Be Present)

Dr. Kaleb Stoppel, CMAA – Kansas (Be Seen)

Jon Payne, CMAA – Ohio (Be Present)

Brian Nolan, CAA – Florida (Do the Job)

Josh Matthews, CMAA – Georgia (Be Present)

Bob Bruglio – Florida – (Be Seen!)

David Marlow, CMAA – Vermont (Have Big Shoulders)

Jen Doede, RAA – Illinois (Be Present)

Dr. Keisha Knowles, CAA – Georgia (Be Intentional)

Ken Edwards, CMAA – Virginia (Be a Leader)

Laura Zamora – Florida (Got to have Grit)

Jim Harris, CMAA – Virginia (Be Visible)

I realize that I have said this a few times already, but it bears repeating – we have shared 14 Categories of Tools so far, ranging from tools that were suggested by just one Athletic Director, all the way up to our most recent tool that was named by 35 AD's.

Regardless of the number of times a particular tool is mentioned, I really want to stress that all these tools are important, and they definitely have their place in The Athletic Director's Toolbox!

Now, it's time to move on to the Top 6 Tools suggested by the interviews from The Educational AD Podcast! Let's Go!

# CHAPTER 15

Tool # 6 – It's All About the Relationships!

How about another offering for our Stat Geeks (Remember - I'm one of them)! Looking back at our first 14 Tools, ranging from #20 (unique tools) and moving up to and including our next tool, #6 ... these tool suggestions account for just under HALF – 233 total mentions - of all the tools that have been suggested and categorized.

Tool #6 – It's All About the Relationships - was a tool that was suggested by 38 of our podcast guests, and it speaks directly to the importance of Building Relationships with the people we serve and those that we work with.

Pam Lancaster, CMAA and Athletic Director at Auburndale High School in Florida said to be sure and "Develop Relationships with your student athletes and your coaches." Pam said she has unfortunately seen schools where "the kids didn't even know who their athletic director was!"

Pam says to, "Engage with the students in the hallways and in the cafeteria, and ... go to practices and go to Band concerts!" She is right! It is all about the Relationships! Make sure this tool is in your toolbox!

John Sgromlo, CAA and Clay County (Florida) District Athletic Director has become a good friend of mine in a very short time! John was one of the presenters for our FIAAA "Virtual" Conference in the spring of 2020 and I was very impressed with his professionalism and his passion!

John's tool contribution here is also about Building Relationships with the people you work alongside of, and he shared, "... there are three people you need to immediately build a positive relationship with and that is your Principal, your Head Custodian, and your Head Book-keeper, "as you're going to be working directly with them "Almost every day!"

I think we can all agree that building a positive Relationship with those three – and the rest of your "Team" – is a great tool to have!

Russell Wambles, CMAA and long-time Florida Athletic

Director who I like call one of my FIAAA "Mentors" also shared "Relationship Building" and he really walks the walk on this one as he serves as the FIAAA's Director of Corporate Sponsorship! Russell has developed quite an impressive number of Corporate Sponsors for our state's organization and continued to nurture these where it is very rare for one of our sponsors to leave us! Russell does a great job of encapsulating this when he says, "People are More Important than Tasks!" He continues by saying, "Focus on the People… you have to do the task – but focus on the people – build your relationships!" It's easy to see why Russell has been so successful! He has the right Tools in his Toolbox! Make sure you do too!

Allison Posey is not an Athletic Director, but she is a great television sports reporter for WTXL/ABC 27 in Tallahassee, Florida and she does a fantastic job of covering high school and college sports in the Florida Panhandle.

One of Allison's tools for Athletic Directors is the importance of building good relationships with everyone, including the media, as most reporters really want to tell the "Good" stories about your teams! Build a good relationship with your local media – it really is a Great Tool for the toolbox!

Kelly Fish, CMAA is he Director of Athletics at Curry Ingram School in Nashville, Tennessee, and someone I get to work with each year at the NIAAA National Conference when we get together at part of the National Faculty for LTI 701, Middle School Programs.

Kelly does a great job with her program and one of her tools – which I placed in this category – came from one of her favorite books, where Jay Bilas was quoting Duke Men's' Basketball Coach, Mike Krzyzewski who said, "You're never Tough Alone."

Kelly says that you need to build those relationships, in part, to make sure you have people who have your back when times are tough! Of course, you are going to be there for them – that's where the "Relationship Building" comes in! I really like that – "You're Never Tough Alone!" What a great tool to have in your Toolbox!

Sheri Stice is a CMAA and a member of the NIAAA's Hall of Fame. The long-time high school Athletic Director from Texas is also active as the NIAAA's Certification Program Director which is where I first met her as a "wide eyed" member of the committee. Sheri really served as a great mentor to me, and she weighs in on the toolbox with her advice to "Infuse every position you supervise with Importance ... from the concession stand worker to the custodian, from the ticket taker ... Every single job is important!"

Sheri continues by suggesting that you "Get in there and do the work with them!" What better way to build trust and those key relationships that allow us to be successful! Make sure this tool is in your toolbox!

Lisa Gingras, CMAA is the Director of Athletics at Nashua High Schools and she's also a member of the NIAAA Board of Directors! Lisa's toolbox idea shows up here with "Building the right relationship with the right people."

Lisa stressed that you need to, "know your facilities person, make sure you have a great secretary ... your bus and transportation people ... and build those relationships with the other Athletic Directors in your area!"

Once again, the importance of building – and maintain – positive relationships with the people whose lives you touch cannot be overstated! Keep this Tool in your toolbox!

Kate Williams is the Assistant Athletic Director at the Catlin Gable School in Portland, Oregon and we had a chance to visit in November of 2020, just as Kate was taking over as the Interim Head Athletic Director. Kate shared her philosophy which included having "a great working relationship and familiarity with your school community."

Kate went on to say, "I was fortunate having gone to school at Catlin and now my own child attends the school ..." but for someone just starting out, "you need to build relationships with grounds or enrollment and admissions and understand how athletics fits in with each department!" Some great advice from a young and talented Athletic Director!

Don Bales, CMAA who is a long time Athletic Director in Indiana who is now working for the NIAAA as the Program Director for Professional Development! Don oversees the NIAAA Committees including Certification, Coaches Education, and LTI as well as directing the State Coordinators meetings each year.

Don's contribution to the Toolbox was another AD who felt Relationship Building was key, stating "learn how to build relationships, because when you build relationships – you build trust – and when you build trust – you build confidence!"

He went on to say that "people might not always agree with you, but if they have a good relationship with you, then they will understand you!" Don Bales is a True Master AD!

In January of 2021, I had a great interview with Sally Ann Reis who is the Founder and CEO of PlayyOn, an online sports management solution for athletic programs and teams. PlayyOn offers a free instant website with registration forms, payment options/forms and scheduling tools, plus a communications dashboard.

With all of that "tech," Sally still stressed the idea of "Camaraderie" and she mentioned the movie Remember The Titans of an example of what "Teamwork can accomplish…"

Sally spoke glowingly of "building relationships with your community through sports." Another example of the need to have THIS tool in your Athletic Director Toolbox!

Dr. Greg Dale of Duke University gets a second mention here for his use of the "tool" which he calls, "Emotional Equity" and shares that "You need to find ways to Fill Up the people you work with!"

I love the visual he shares of "filling up a tank" – Greg also uses the term "Make Deposits" which we have already heard. Dr. Greg Dale really has some wonderful ideas – some wonderful "tools" – that need to go into every Athletic Director's Toolbox!

Flynn Baliton is a student-athlete at Father Lopez Catholic School in Daytona Beach, Florida and during one of our Student Panel Interviews she shared her thoughts – "I think AD's should try and connect with their athletes … it's all about the relationships."

Sometimes as Athletic Directors move away from coaching their own teams, it can be challenging to make and keep those connections with the students. Here is an outstanding student and student athlete reminding us all that it's about the Relationships!

Josh Scott, CMAA is the Athletic Director for The Springfield, Missouri School District along with being the long-time Secretary for the NIAAA Board of Directors.

Josh had some interesting tools to suggest and here we have his suggestion of "Building Personal Connections and Relationships..." and he suggests that you "Don't text someone every time you have a question or a problem," but rather, "Pick up the phone and call people!"

Josh suggests using an "old time rotary phone..." but in the absence of that, use your cell phone and call someone! A novel idea – using your phone to actually talk to someone! I challenge you to put this tool into your toolbox.

Other Athletic Directors from The Educational AD podcast interviews who have previously contributed to the Toolbox Top Twenty, and who also shared this tool include -

Jay Getty, CAA – Florida (Relationships)

Jen Brooks, CMAA – Missouri (Be Approachable)

Ernest Roberson, Jr. CMAA – Florida (Positive Relationships)

Steve McHale, CAA – Florida (Family Atmosphere)

Rebecca Moe – Washington (Learn everyone's name)

Amanda Waters, CAA – Georgia (Relationships)

Rich Barton, CMAA – Utah (Reach Out)

Nathan Stanley, CAA – Oregon (Be a Servant Leader)

Dan Schuster, CMAA – Indiana (Send Thank You Cards)

Jamie Sheetz, CMAA – Utah (Connect with People)

Kristin Peeples, CAA – Florida (Relationships)

Quante Speight, CAA – North Carolina (Be a Servant Leader)

Don Baker, CAA – Georgia (Relationships)

Jen Doede, RAA – Illinois (Relationships)

Rob Seymour, CMAA –

John Beau Drake – North Carolina (Relationships)

Brian Nolan, CAA – Florida (Write Thank You Notes)

Teg Cosgriff, CMAA – Connecticut (Be a Servant Leader)

Emily Barkley, CMAA – Oklahoma (Relationships)

Annette Scogin, CMAA – Arkansas (Relationships)

Doug Stephens – Florida (Be a Servant Leader)

Shea Collins, CAA – North Carolina (Hand out "Gift Cards")

Cassidy Lichtman – California (You Must Care!)

Next up – Our Top 5 Toolbox Categories!

# CHAPTER 16

Tool # 5 – <u>Balancing Your AD Life</u>

Continuing with our Statistics - Our first 15 Tool Categories contained just under HALF (233 total mentions) of the total number of tool suggestions we received from our Athletic Director interviews.

As we move into the Top 5 Categories of Tools, the suggestions we received make up 51% of all the Toolbox suggestions we received. Yes, these tools were mentioned more frequently than the others, but I want to again emphasize that ALL of our toolbox "tools" should be considered important, and that each Athletic Director needs to find – and use – the best tools for their school setting.

We will continue with the countdown now with Tool # 5 – Balancing Your Life. We had 39 AD's share the importance of having a Balance between work and home, job and family, and Life in general! The tool of "Balance" along with "Self-Care" were the most frequent, along with Eating Right, Getting enough Sleep, and Exercising.

Tyrone McGriff, CAA and the Athletic Director at the Florida State University School in Tallahassee, Florida shows up in the Toolbox at #5 as he emphasizes the importance of "Sleep!" Coach McGriff says, "You're going to be dealing with a lot of issues and you need to be able relax and recharge," so you can be at your best!
Tyrone is going to need his sleep because as we go to print, he and his wife have just added child number two! Get some Sleep in your Toolbox!

Mike Ostrowski, CAA and the Director of Athletics at North Broward Prep School in Coconut Creek, Florida. Mike and I got to work together on the FHSAA Athletic Director Advisory Committee, and I found him to be a real Pro at administration!
Mike suggests that you keep "a couple of granola bars as a meal replacement" because you are going to miss a "few" meals and "also

have a metaphorical alarm-clock to remind you when it's time to take a break!" Taking care of yourself and finding nutritional "balance" is a great tool to have in your toolbox!

One of my favorite interviews had to be with Misty Buck, who has taken her experiences as an elite athlete and coach and written a book called The Athlete Mental Health Playbook. Misty feels that managing mental wellness truly takes an "ongoing mind, body, and soul holistic plan..." which is why she suggested putting her book into the toolbox!

Misty correctly points out that "Mental Health and Mental Training are already part of the narrative and the need to be versed in this is only going to increase!"

Misty also adds that to truly help a someone, "You need to look at them holistically." Pick up a copy of The Athlete Mental Health Playbook and add it to your Athletic Director Toolbox!

Lynn Flint, CAA is the Director of Athletics at Haddam Killingworth High School in Connecticut and I first met her when we were co-presenters at the NIAAA Conference on How to Help Struggling Coaches.

Lynn does a fantastic job at her school, and she added to the toolbox with her suggestion to have some kind of "strategy ... such as meditation, to help counter stress."

Lynn also says that "...after one of those days, having a tool like a meditation or yoga or going for a run to say, OK, that part of the day is over..." to help relieve the stress because – and Lynn is spot on correct with this, "A stressed Athletic Director is a help to No One!" Find your Balance with one of these great tools that Lynn suggests!

Cheryl Shivel is an award-winning Athletic Director who directs the programs at Astronaut High School in Titusville, Florida. Cheryl is a self-described "Old School" Athletic Director, and one of her three AD toolbox suggestions definitely falls into this category of Balancing Your AD Life (Self Care!).

Cheryl says you need to "Keep a Cooler of your Favorite soda nearby..." along with "a good meditation exercise" to make sure the stress of the job – and yes, there IS stress – does not get in the way of doing your very best! I agree with Cheryl wholeheartedly about the cooler! Make sure your Toolbox is stocked accordingly!

Monica Maxwell, CMAA and Athletic Director at East Central Chicago High School in Indiana is one of several former WNBA players I have interviewed who are now AD's. Monica does a great job at her school, and she shared the tool of "Finding Balance" by suggesting that you, "Take a Vacation!"

Monica said, "We spend so many late nights and weekends on this job that you have to take care of your health ... you have those vacation days so make sure you take them!" This advice is coming from one of the hardest working Athletic Directors that I know! Make sure you have this tool in your Toolbox and use it!

Meg Seng, CMAA is the outstanding Director of Athletics at the Greenhill School in Ann Arbor, Michigan, and we worked together as members of the NIAAA Certification Committee.

Meg is one of the top Athletic Directors in our profession and she is also the co-founder of The Academy of Sports Leadership (TASL), a non-profit organization that provides education and training for women interested in becoming coaches and leaders.

Meg also appears in this tool category with her suggestion to "establish systems to take care of yourself... we talk so much about mental health so set some boundaries to sleep better and eat better, and you'll find you feel a lot better!"

Meg was always a leader on our Certification Committee, and she shows her leadership here! Take some time and create those "systems" for your toolbox!

The great Ed Lockwood, CMAA out of North Dakota is up next in the Toolbox Top Twenty Countdown! Ed is another Hall of Fame AD, and he currently serves as the Assistant Program Director for the NIAAA Certification Program.

In addition to being a coach and Athletic Director over his career, Ed also served as the Executive Director for the North Dakota AD Association! One of his contributions to the Toolbox is to "Understand you have a family, learn to communicate with them!"

Ed stressed that "Quality family Time was key," and it should be "Uninterrupted by TV, phones, or other distractions!" He finished by stating "You need to be purposeful about scheduling quality family time ... as it will become the most important thing you do for your own emotional health!"

Looking back at my own kids and our family time, I think we did a pretty good job, but I also know it could (should) have been a lot better! Please take Ed's advice and make sure THIS tool is in your Athletic Director's Toolbox!

Courtnay Windemaker is a CAA and the Director of Athletics at Tenoroc High School in Lakeland, Florida. Courtnay is one of the rising stars in our state and she shared from her own experience the need to "Keep a Balance between work and home life," saying, "… a few years ago, I burned myself out by coaching two sports, being the Athletic Director…and working with clients."

Courtnay added, "I had to step away, but I eventually realized how much I missed it and fortunately had the opportunity to come back at another school." Courtnay really emphasized, "Remember to take sure you make time for yourself!"

Dr. Mekia Troy, CAA is the Athletic Director at Creekside High School in Douglasville, Georgia. For one of her toolbox tool suggestions, Dr. Troy encouraged us to "Find something that will help you Clock Out…" saying, "You have to be able to step away and decompress … you will come back better for it!"

She continued, sharing "We talk about Time Management all the time, but Time Management also includes Energy Management as well!" In all the things we do as Athletic Directors, Dr. Troy hits it on the head when she reminds us to have THIS tool in our Athletic Director Toolbox!

Several years ago, I was an AD in California, and I got to know Stevi Balsamo who is a CAA and Athletic Director at Millennium High School in Tracey, California.

Stevi always did a great job with her teams, and here she offers her Toolbox suggestions here with the tool of "Have a set End Time to your day," which is something she says she is still learning how to do!

She reminds us that "There are things that can wait until tomorrow – not everything is an emergency, not everything needs to get done today…"

Stevi also suggests "It's OK to put your phone on Sleep Mode," and step away from it! Another great idea – a great tool – to have in your Athletic Director Toolbox!

Lisa McCullough, CMAA is the Assistant Athletic Director at The Bush School in Seattle and she also brings the perspective of having been an International School Athletic Director for several years.

One of Lisa's toolbox tools was "Time Management," not just for the job but also as it applies to your physical and mental health. She also shared that her school is very proactive - for students and for teachers and coaches - in the areas of Diversity and Equity, which is certainly and important aspect of mental health.

As we continue with the countdown, obviously we will see MORE Athletic Director mentioning these final five tools, and we definitely want to acknowledge their choices. Here are the Athletic Directors who shared "Finding a Balance" as one of their Top 3 Tools —

John Sgromolo, CAA – Florida (Exercise)

Becky Moran, CMAA – Illinois (Self Care)

Pete Shambo, CMAA – New York (Balance)

Jessica Upchurch, CAA – Florida (Balance)

Joey Struwe, CMAA – South Dakota (Balance)

Dixie Wescott, CMAA – Missouri (Balance)

Dan Comeau, CMAA – Florida (Balance)

Dr. Lisa Langston, CMAA – Texas (Self Care)

Jason Frey, CAA – Florida (Energy!)

Nicole Ebsen, CAA – Illinois (Balance)

Dr. Kaleb Stoppel, CMAA – Kansas (Balance)

Tara Osborne, CAA – Alabama (Self Care)

Dr. Dustin Smith, CMAA – Arkansas (Balance)

Amber O'Malley, CAA – Florida (Balance)

Jamie Sheetz, CMAA – Utah (Self Care)

Sally Ann Reis – California (Vacation!)

Mike McGurk, CMAA – Missouri (Balance)

Susan Noonan – Texas (Self Care)

Josh Matthews, CMAA – Georgia (Faith & Devotion)

Jackie Randall, CAA – Illinois (Have a Meal Planner)

Rob Seymour, CMAA – Indiana (Balance)

Jen Doede, RAA – Illinois (Breathe!)

Marc "Hutch" Hunter, CMAA – Utah (Self Care)

Lacey London, CAA – Washington (Balance)

Teg Cosgriff, CMAA – Connecticut (Breathe!)

Emily Barkley, CMAA – Oklahoma (Balance)

Josh Scott, CMAA – Missouri (Nights Out with Spouse)

Darryl Nance, CMAA – South Carolina (Family!)


These Athletic Directors all felt that Balance – including Exercise, Self-Care, Nutrition, Sleep, Breathing, Vacations, and Family Time were important Tools to have in your Athletic Director Toolbox!

To paraphrase that well known credit card commercial ... "What's in Your Toolbox?

# CHAPTER 17

Tool # 4 – Communication

Next up, 44 of our Athletic Directors said "Communication" was an important tool and this should come as no surprise. Some of the AD's mentioned "One on One communication" with coaches, kids, parents, and stakeholders – while others focused on just one aspect like "Keeping your principal informed" or "Meeting regularly w/coaches."

Some of our Athletic Directors also shared the importance of having your cell phone at the ready, along with using the written word to communicate.

As previously mentioned, we will continue to see a lot more of our interview guests repeated as they listed these Top 4 tools in their toolbox, so let's take a look at how – and why – so many of our Athletic Directors listed Communication as one of their most important Toolbox Tools!

Michael Colby was the very first Athletic Director in Florida to earn the CMAA designation and he has had a Hall of Fame career as an AD, as a Director for the Florida High School Athletic Association, and as a long-time member of the FIAAA Board where he currently organizes the Vendors and their Booths for our annual conference.

Mike shares the importance of Communication, saying that AD's should be, "Communicating with Coaches and their Athletes, as well as with a mentor (see our following tools!) to know what they should be doing that day…"

Mike continued, saying "I did just that with the new AD's that came on board down in Miami - Dade County … setting up one on one meetings with them to make sure they were up to date on everything ranging from the county to the state."

I still recall speaking with Mike my first year in Florida and I can attest to his wisdom and diligence in helping Communicate the important tasks for an Athletic Director!

Next, we hear from Nicole Norris, CAA and Director of

Athletics at East Lansing High School in East Lansing, Michigan. Nicole says to "create a system where you can improve your communication skills."

Nicole said that "This is tough but find something that works for you." Nicole uses an "Excel Spreadsheet that's up on my wall that shows every event ... and is color coded, but that is what works for me!"

Tammie Talley, CAA is the County AD for Duval County in Florida along with serving as the FIAAA's Board Secretary. Tammie led off with the suggestion of, "Communicating with your Principal, your coaches, ... your parents," and she said don't always communicate with them in the same way, instead "use a variety of ways including email, texting, and calls along with apps that link particular groups – such as GroupMe – and turn the notifications on!"

Holly Farnese, CMAA also had Communication as one of her Top 3 Tools. Holly has done such as great job with the NIAAA's Leadership Training Program as the Lead Instructor for the two Middle School LTI courses. From Creating and Editing to Revising and Presenting, she does an outstanding job of communicating with her team of instructors!

Steve Ripley, CMAA is on the FIAAA Board as the Director of Public Relations so it should be no surprise that Communication was one of his most important Tools!

Steve came in with "Get to know your coaches ... Meet with each of them individually and let them share what they need from you to be successful!"

Amanda Waters, CAA and Athletic Director at St. Andrews School in Savannah, Georgia also put Communication in the Athletic Director's Toolbox.

Amanda said, "You have to meet with everyone and Communicate with everyone!" Her advice would include, "Have a checklist of everyone you need to communicate with."

Russell Wambles, CMAA is another member of our FIAAA Board, handling our very successful Corporate Sponsorship

Program and he also stressed the importance of having Communication in your Toolbox.

"Bring all of the Stakeholders together ..." was part of Russell's take on Communication, as he said, "You need everyone to be on board if we're going to achieve our goals of giving our student athletes the best opportunity to achieve in life!" The ability to Communicate Has to take in everyone's perspective!"

Carol Dozibrin is a CMAA and the Executive Director of the New Hampshire Athletic Directors Association. Carol also had Communication in her toolbox saying, "Communicate, Communicate, Communicate!"

She continued with this thought saying, "Don't be afraid to ask questions so you don't end up trying to re-invent the wheel!" Good Stuff! Communicate applies in both directions!

Dr. Danielle LaPointe of Manatee High School in Bradenton, Florida said that for her, the # 1 Tool was Communication. She said, "Communicating with your coaches is important, and a big part of that communication includes Coaching your Coaches!"

She added, "Coaches need to know how to communicate with their players, how to talk with an angry parent, or how to remain professional with the media after a tough loss and we are not doing our jobs as AD's if we are not communicating with our Coaches."

We also heard from the "Bow Tie AD," Doug Killgore, CMAA who is another Hall of Fame Athletic Director we got to interview!

Doug encouraged us to Communicate this way, saying "Don't be afraid to ask for help, and he added, "We as AD's are totally willing to share what we have with you ... Unlike most coaches, who don't want to share anything because they think you will use it to beat them in a ballgame!"

Doug concluded his tool with, "Anything I have as an Athletic Director, I am willing to give you if it will make your job easier!"

Mary Walker is the AD at Fernandina Beach High School on Amelia Island in the very Northeast corner of Florida and she shared the following nugget about Communication, saying "Get a Bullhorn and Communicate with your Coaches!"

She continued, saying "Coaches want to know, they want to do things right … so have a plan and communicate it to them!"

Ann Stewert, CAA and Director of Athletics at New Mexico's Los Alamos High School offered up "Communicate and Listen" saying, "Listening is so important, but then … make sure you go and communicate with your coaches, your athletes, and your administrators … make sure everyone is on the same page."
Ann added this – "If you're not talking with your coaches, you might have someone end up going off the deep end (I would call this Going Rogue) …" so to avoid this, make sure Communication is part of your Toolbox!

Josh Blumenthal is the very successful Head Lacrosse Coach and Assistant Athletic Director at St. Andrews Episcopal School in Austin, Texas and he shared a specific example of Communication with this –
"Parents don't mind when there are schedule changes as long as they know what's going on…" adding, "communicating those changes allows them to stay up to date and stay excited about attending your events!"

Mike McGurk, CMAA makes another appearance in the Toolbox Top Twenty! Mike is the AD at Lee's Summit High School in Missouri and the current NIAAA President Elect, and he shares "Number one, the ability to communicate with everyone is critical," adding "…that includes the custodian, the secretaries, and the coaches!"
Mike also said Communication was not just schedules and details but "Communicate that you truly Value everyone on your Athletic Team!"

Jackie Randall, CAA from El Grove High School in Illinois contributed one of our "Unique" tools in Chapter one, and she also came up with one of our top 4 tools sharing, "Have a cell phone or a walkie-talkie because Communication is huge!"
She added, "You also need to be able to effectively communicate with all of your stakeholders…" and "you need to be pro-active and aware of the many different people that you have relationships with and have to communicate with!"

Josh Wilson is also a repeat contributor with the tool of Communication which, again, should come as no surprise coming from the publisher of FloridaHSFootball.com where he has over 50,000 followers on Twitter!

Josh shares this, saying "Keep People Engaged on Your Social Media Platform." Josh spoke at length about Twitter, Facebook, and Instagram but suggested "I think Instagram might be best because people love photos … and Instagram gives fans a connection to your program."

Some wise words from a Communications Pro! Make sure this tool is somewhere in your Athletic Director Toolbox!

Kari Avila, CAA from Arizona's Salome High School shares the tool of Communication with "You have to Communicate with your Coaches and your Administration," adding "Your administration does not want to be surprised by anything!"

Kari also said, "People are going to look to you for answers, and while you might not always have them, but if you're genuine and truthful, they will trust you to find out … because you have been open with them and you have communicated that they can trust you!"

Antony Fisher, CMAA and Athletic Director for the Minneapolis Public School District also had Communication in his toolbox, and he shared his ideas through a "3 Year Business Model" approach.

The model itself can apply to Roster or Team Size, Wins and Losses, Budgets or Fundraising, or any other area but essentially, the 3 years apply as follows -

Tony explains as follows, "In year one, expect a loss, and then in year two you should break even, and then in year three you should see a profit."

Using scheduling and competition as an example, he says "Year one, you create a schedule where you know you have a chance to win about half of your games … and then in year two you see improvement, so you schedule a few tougher opponents, but the plan is to break even …"

He continued, saying "In year three, you've become strong enough to feel confident that you're going to have a winning season." Tony said this could apply to the number of teams you offer such as maybe, "year one, you just have a varsity team. Then in year two you add a JV Team, and then in year three you have two solid programs, and you can add a freshman team (or middle school)."

Tony also shared the importance of revisiting the plan and also sharing the plan (Communicating) with your administration. This is a really good example of how the tool of Communication can work for you!

We always had a great time with our Student Panel Interviews and the one featuring two student athletes from Maryland was a great one! Patrick Hayburn and Hope Davis from St. Mary's High School in Annapolis, both hit on aspects of using the tool of Communication with Patrick saying "you need to communicate the excitement of athletics to everyone in the school..." while Hope spoke of "engaging the community" by getting the word out regarding games.

Melanie Redd is the Director of Melanie Redd Performance Training, and she emphasized the importance of "An open line of communication between athletes, coaches, and administration..." and "I think everyone thrives when the communication level is high, and everyone is on the same page ..."

As an off-campus provider, Melanie often finds herself as the "Communicator" between two head Coaches at the same school for things like weight room time and training, so she has become adept at using this tool!

Make sure you have Communication in your Athletic Director Toolbox!

Ken Edwards, CMAA who is the athletic director at Jamestown High School in Williamsburg, Virginia says Communication is, "an evolving trait because once you think you've mastered it, that is probably a sign you're falling behind!"

He continues, saying "There are so many platforms, from social media to communicating on the telephone ... but the best way is face to face..." and he added this point, "Don't be afraid to – and learn how to – have those hard conversations!"

Ken understands the importance of being a great communicator. Make sure this tool is one you learn how to use effectively!

Laura Zamora is a senior manager at City Year in Miami, Florida where she works with schools to train the next generation of leaders. Laura contributes to the toolbox with the need to "Communicate your vision to your stakeholders..." along with, "You are a key member of the school, and you'll need to connect with people and build bridges..."

Next, we hear from another Virginia Athletic Director – Jim Harris, CMAA who is the AD at T.C. Williams High School which many of you will recall as the setting for the famous move "Remember the Titans."

Jim's AD toolbox contribution includes the tool of "Authentic Communication," meaning "You should communicate as much as you can – don't keep it to yourself – to as many people as you can!"

Jim continued his thought, saying "... its critical, especially when you are starting out, to share as much of the information you have as possible, to keep everyone on the same page!"

Chris Hall, CMAA and Director of Athletics at Discovery High in Lawrenceville, Georgia. Chris already contributed to the toolbox with his unique tool of "Kill Your Own Snakes" to describe helping your coaches solve some of their own problems.

He returns here with the need to use "Effective Communication..." saying, "I've learned to consider who my audience is what exactly it is that I've trying to communicate."

Chris also shared he feels it's important "to also get to really know your coaches."

Other Athletic Directors who put the tool of Communication in their Toolbox were:

Rocky Gillis, CAA – Florida

Sheri Stice, CMAA - Texas

Allison Posey – Florida

Dan Schuster, CMAA - Indiana

Wayne Stofsky – Florida

Stacey Segal, CMAA - Texas

**Dr.** Chris Hobbs, CMAA – Florida

Lisa Gingras, CMAA – New Hampshire

Mike Ostrowski, CAA – Florida

Don Bales, CMAA - Indiana

Dan Comeau, CMAA – Florida

Misty Buck – Florida

David Marlow, CMAA - Vermont

Cheryl Shivel – Florida

Pam Cawley, CAA – Florida

Lisa McCullough, CMAA - Washington

Kelly Blount, CAA - Florida

Mary Walker – Florida

Jason Frey, CAA – Florida

As you can see, Communication was a very popular choice as a much-needed tool for any Athletic Director!

Now, we're moving on to the **TOP THREE TOOLS** as suggested for the Athletic Director's Toolbox!

# CHAPTER 18

Tool # 3 – <u>Organization</u>

Coming in just ahead of Communication was Organization which appeared 45 times. Together, these two tools represented 21% of all of the tool suggestions in the Toolbox!

Some of the ways our Athletic Directors expressed this was suggesting that we "Keep a Planner," and several said they still use an old-school written plan book (I know I do!).

Others talked about keeping everything that an AD needs on some kind of spread sheet including schedules, calendars, contacts, and the like.

It goes without saying that Athletic Directors need to have some kind of Organizational system to keep all of the "Balls they Juggle" from hitting the ground – I like the phrase "Juggling Flaming Chain Saws" better but that's another story!

Let's get Organized!

Leading off we have Jay Getty, CAA from Hagerty High School in Florida who is not only a great AD but also a National caliber XC Coach and one of the FIAAA gurus with all things related to Twitter and other forms of social media.

Jay mentioned the importance of "Getting ahead of the Day" and to do that, "you have to be organized!" Jay has a routine that he shares of "getting up and running, then updating social media posts for the school … and then going to school, often times for parking lot supervision!" THAT is what being organized is all about!

John Sgromolo, CAA and the Clay County (Florida) Athletic Director, shared the importance of having "a Planner, a Calendar, a Scheduler to make you effective with time management!"

He continued – "You're going to have so many people clamoring for your attention that if you don't have a planner, it will become overwhelming very fast!" John's point is not to scare you, but to "motivate and prepare you for the job… Start Planning!"

Ron Allan is the Athletic Director at Lecanto High School in Central Florida and he's also on our FIAAA Board. Ron says, "You don't know what you don't know!" so having some kind of organizational plan allows you to learn and begin to "know what you need to know!"

Ron mentions the need to, "...utilize Athletic Director checklists that allow you to keep the important items in front of you!' He added, "The FIAAA publishes these along with other organizations, and you can use them or tweak them to fit your school."

Ron is spot on – check your own state association's website and search "Athletic Director Checklist." Add THAT tool to your toolbox!

Stephanie Blackwell, CMAA is the state and national award-winning Athletic Director at Bixby High School in Oklahoma and she's also a hard-working member of the NIAAA's Certification Committee.

Stephanie suggests you need to be "very organized" and used her school's Covid response as an example. Stephanie shared how the "district has created our plan based on the policies and regulations that we have been presented with (by the state) and we're moving forward."

Obviously, that takes a LOT of planning and organization at multiple levels! Make sure you practice using your "Organization" tool in your toolbox!

Allison Fondale, CMAA and AD at St. Mary's High School in Annapolis, Maryland makes another appearance at Tool #4. Allison shares that she needs a "Calendar or Google Calendar so you can prioritize instead of falling victim to trying to do Everything!"

She said, "You have to prioritize on a daily and a weekly basis..." adding, "... you really need to have it on your cell phone!"

With apps and ready-made programs, it's much easier to get organized! Put this tool in your Athletic Director Toolbox!

Dr. Chris Hobbs, CMAA is the very successful AD at The King's Academy in Palm Beach County, Florida and also one of the most prolific readers and Tweeter/Bloggers that I know!

Chris is really on top of all things AD related, and he shares his thoughts on AD Organization, saying "I really recommend the **rschooltoday** program as a management system … as it really helps you to organize transportation, game schedules, coach's certifications, and even scores."

There are a lot of systems out there by Dr. Hobbs really believes in this one as he says, "It's not expensive and it will set you up to organize your program."

You NEED to get Organized – find a platform or a system that you can put into your Athletic Director Toolbox!

Mike Ostrowski, CAA and Director of Athletics at Coconut Creek's North Broward Prep School in South Florida also makes another appearance. Mike has Organization as one of his Top Three Tools saying, "You have to be organized and understand that events are going to happen and that you are in charge!"

Mike also says that being organized also allows you to enjoy some time off by scheduling your "down time" along with your school related events.

Dan Comeau, CMAA is the FIAAA Director of Mentoring and the man I credit with getting me involved with our state association back in 2008. Dan also had Organization in his toolbox stating, "the thing that helped me most was a HUGE white board in my office… and I had it there for 25 years."

He continued, "we had our schedules on it and if there was a change, it got changed on the White Board FIRST!" Dan says some kind of "Planner is very important to have at your fingertips!"

Like I said, Dan is my FIAAA Mentor and if says Organization is important – I believe him, and so should you!

Mark Lee, CAA is the Athletic Director at Hernando High School in Brooksville, Florida and he shares his Organizational tool as a "Google Calendar on your phone…" because there are just "so many things you need to keep track of that you can't write all of them down!"

Mark also shared that "we don't have administrative assistants, so the Google Calendar is critical to keep us organized."

Marcus Gabriel, CAA is the Athletic Director at American High School in Hialeah, Florida and also the 2021 President Elect for the

FIAAA. Marcus' organization tool is a reminder to "Manage your day…" saying "I get to the office early every day, so I have an hour of uninterrupted time to plan!"

Marcus adds "If you don't plan appropriately, you're going to fail!" Make sure YOU plan!

Chris Fore, CAA is the Principal at Palmdale Aerospace Academy in California, but he was also a highly successful Head Football Coach and Athletic Director, and he also founded and directs EightLaces.com consulting.

Chris shared that his own "Athletic Director Manual" from his website, "or any resource that has forms or documents for facilities, transportation, hiring …" to help an Athletic Director find an "organization system or philosophy that every athletic director needs."

Make sure you check out Chris's website and get Organized!

Jonathan Bukva is a CMAA and the Athletic Director at Ronald Regan Middle School in Manassas, Virginia. I got to know Jonathan through the NIAAA Portal (check it out) and had a chance to help him with his great CMAA project!

He shared his thoughts on the importance of Organization with the suggestion of "Making a Task List that says, here is what you need to do …" and then he related how that helped him complete his CMAA project." A task list is a great tool!

Monica Maxwell, CMAA shows up again with the Organizational Tool. Monica is the AD at East Central Chicago High School in Indiana, and she says, "the number one thing you better have is a Calendar because no two days are alike!"

She continued saying, "the calendar keeps you organized, so you won't miss anything!" There are many ways to get organized – find the organizational tool that works best for you, and then use it!

Anne Julian, CAA is the Director of Athletics at Holy Cross High School in Covington, Kentucky. Anne previously appeared in the Toolbox countdown at Tool # 11 with her book suggestion – Happy Kids Don't Punch You in the Face!

Anne also had Organization in her toolbox, saying "you need to have a Flip Calendar that goes on a file basket… and in the file are the things that need to be done that month."

Anne also mentioned earlier that you "should never handle a piece of paper more than twice…" which I think can also go into this part of the toolbox!

Nicole Ebsen is a CAA and the Athletic Director at Morton High School in Berwyn, Illinois. Nicole has already contributed tools to the toolbox but she is back with this tool saying, "You need to have a good Scheduling Tool…" adding "I don't always use technology, so I have a huge scheduling binder…"

Nicole also said, "Get a system that works for you to schedule and stick to it to help you stay organized."

By her own admission, her planner is "Old School," but it can be anything that allows you to get, and stay, organized!

Sally Ann Reis, the Founder and CEO of PlayyOn, an online sports management solution makes another appearance in the Athletic Director's Toolbox. Sally Ann, of course, suggested that AD's should use her PlayyOn platform which, "is free to sign up for," and added "you have all the tools of scheduling and communication for coaches, student athletes, parents, and fans!"

Check out the PlayyOn app at www.playyon.com It's a great way to put the tool of Organization into your Athletic Director Toolbox!

Shay Steele is the Assistant Athletic Director at Walnut Hills H.S. in Cincinnati, Ohio and even as a younger AD, she knows the importance of being Organized.

Shay said, "you need to have a Planner to keep track of all of your meetings, deadlines, and schedules." She also said, "The Planner and a PEN go hand in hand…" so make sure you have your pen with you!

Jay Hammes, CMAA is most well known for being the Founder of **SAFESPORTZONE**, but he has also been involved in athletics his entire life as a student-athlete, as a coach, and as a teacher and athletic administrator, both at the high school, district level and collegiate level.

Jay's toolbox also has Organization in it, stating the importance of "staying current, and Planning doesn't cost anything!" He continued saying, "Safesport has developed a free Afterschool Safety

Assessment for you school." He continued, saying "take your team including your Athletic Trainer, a Coach, Security Officer, and a principal ... and go through your facility," adding "by going through the assessment step by step, checking off the boxes, you end up with an Audit of your facility."

Jay says that being "Prepared is being Organized," and this is so true! Check out the services and programs available, many of them at no cost, on www.safesportzone.com

Lyle Livingood, CAA and the Director of Athletics at West Port High School in Ocala, Florida also suggested Organization as one of his Top Three Tools, stating, "No one is good at anything, until it becomes easy..." adding "You also have to understand that there are timelines – lines in the sand – such as physicals and paperwork, so be as prepared as you can throughout the year."

Lyle does a great job at his school and for the FIAAA Board where he serves as a District Director. He is also highly organized so he definitely Talks the Talk and he Walks the Walk! Make sure Organization is in your Athletic Director Toolbox!

Dr. Kechia Rowles, CAA and is not just the Athletic Director at Rockdale County Schools (GA) but she also serves as the school's Athletic Trainer! Dr. Rowles shared Organization as one of her main tools which comes as no surprise, as she said -

"I'm a planner, so have a check list – have a plan – which makes you optimize your time, and it also makes you accessible and more productive!"

Organization is important enough as an Athletic Director and doubly important if you're also working as the Trainer! Either way, make sure you have Organization in your Athletic Director Toolbox!

Jerri Kelly, CAA is Director of Athletics at Lake Brantley High School in Altamonte Springs, Florida and she also presents an annual workshop at our FIAAA Conference called "The New AD's Toolbox", so she is very familiar with packing tools in a toolbox!

Jerri's toolbox includes Organization, and she tells why, saying "I'm still a Write It Down person so I find my Planner ... I find if I write it down, I remember it."

She also said, "I plan my week with officials, busses, the scoreboard and everything else ... if you plan it out ahead you won't end up dealing with an emergency on game day!" Jerri keeps her planners from previous years as well to use as a resource for repeat events like tournaments and playoffs.

Next, we hear from Teresa Gunter who is the Athletic Director at Tallahassee's Leon High School in the Florida Panhandle. Teresa shares her Organizational Tool Philosophy as follows –

"You need to have some kind of Organizational Plan," sharing that when she took over the job at Leon, the previous AD "had a collection of folders that she had created to help her stay organized." Teresa shared that those folders allowed her to excel in the job and also served as a guide for her own folders.

She also offered this, saying "I always told myself I would never have a paper calendar but here I am using a planner along with the technology because it helps make you organized!"

Teresa also "plans" her email and phone time to help her stay organized and continue to excel at the job!

Mark Rosenbalm, CMAA is the Collier County (Florida) District Athletic Coordinator and he's also a member of our FIAAA Board of Directors. Mark also has a quite the record as a Wrestling Coach here in Florida and his contribution to the toolbox is as follows –

"… Manage all Meetings - don't go in there without a plan and a set of rules or it will get out of hand quickly, and you will never get it back!" Part of Mark's Organization plan dealt with "Chain of Command:" stating "Parents and Coaches knew that they could not talk with me until they had gone to the coach," and the coaches really appreciated that.

Whatever your Plan or Chain of Command is, make sure you have a Plan and that everyone is "in on it!" Be Organized!

Bob Bruglio is the very successful Athletic Director at Port Charlotte High School in Port Charlotte, Florida. Bob placed the tool of Organization in his Toolbox, stating "Try to become the best organizer you can and if you're lucky enough to have an Athletic Secretary – Utilize them!"

He continued saying, "we're not all great sitting behind the desk so if you have that person to help with communication and phone calls, use them to help prevent you from getting overwhelmed."

Other AD's placing Organization in their Toolbox included –

Rocky Gillis, CAA – Florida

Kate Williams - Oregon

Alison Posey – Florida

Julie Renner, CAA - Ohio

Wayne Stofsky – Florida

Holly Farnese, CMAA – Pennsylvania

Scott Drabczyk, CAA – Florida

Moe Orr - California

Casey Thiele, CAA – Florida

Amanda Waters, CAA – Georgia

Deb Margolis - Florida

Becky Moran, CMAA – Illinois

Tim Leeseburg, CAA - Florida

Lynn Flint, CAA – Connecticut

Cheryl Shivel – Florida

Josh Bulmenthal – Texas

Lisa McCullough, CMAA – Washington

Michael Harrison, CAA – Florida

Melanie Redd – Ohio

Stevi Balsamo, CAA – California

Altogether, a total of 45 Athletic Directors out of our 150 Podcast Interviews who selected Organization as one of their Top 3 Tools! It is clear that our podcast guests feel that Athletic Directors need to be Organized!

And then, there were two ...

But before we share the **Top Two** Toolbox Tools, let's share some more statistics -

Our final Two Toolbox Tools appeared on 51 and 63 of our Podcast Guest's most important tools which means together, they represent almost **25%** of the 475 total suggestions.

As you read through the responses for these two Categories, you might feel the two could have been combined into one big category and I agree!
There is definitely a connected theme for these "tools" but in the end I separated them into two concepts that fit my ear and vision. You can certainly disagree with the categories I have chosen, but I think you will agree that as tools, they ALL belong in the Toolbox!

Finally, I want to emphasize - **One More Time** - that while these two answers were the **Most Frequent** suggestions, we really feel that **ALL of the Tools** mentioned have **VALUE**, and that everyone listening needs to find the **"Right SET of Tools"** that will work best for You and Your School!

Now, let's get to the **Top TWO Tools** ...

# CHAPTER 19

Tool # 2 – **Get Involved, and Be a Life-Long Learner**

This Tool was suggested a total of 51 times, and it was expressed in a couple of different ways – the most frequent was "Get Involved with the NIAAA" along with "Get Involved right away with your State Athletic Director Association."

The key phrase was "Get Involved," which was stated 27 times! In this category we also heard from Athletic Directors about the need to continue seek "Professional Development" along with striving to be a "Continual" or a "Life-Long Learner."

Let's GET INVOLVED AND see which Athletic Directors placed this tool in their Toolbox.

First, we have Ron Allan from Lecanto High School in Central Florida. Ron stressed the importance of "Get involved with FIAAA and get involved with FACA (Florida Athletic Coaches Association) and get involved with your professional organizations!"
Ron shared that his "mentors encouraged me … made me get involved!" There is no question that this tool is key to the success of any Athletic Director.

Next, we hear from Kiesha Brown, CMAA and the K-8 Athletic Director at The Galloway School in Atlanta, Georgia. Kiesha is a former Pro Basketball Player (WNBA and Europe) and she also runs a successful business called Bankshot Basketball.
Kiesha shares her tool for this chapter by saying you need to, "Have the willingness and humility for continuous learning … and remain a Life-long Learner…" adding "I think I've learned more on the job than I ever did in school."

Steve McHale, CAA and the Director of Athletics at Dr. Phillips High School in Orlando offers this tool, saying "get involved with FIAAA and NIAAA … take a few LTI courses and go to a conference … get to know people that way and network."
Steve also served our country as a United States Marine, and he brings a sense of hard work, duty, and honor to the job he does at

his school – THANK YOU for your service!

Tol Gropp CMAA and the Director of Athletics at Boise's Timberline High school says, "… I would tell every AD to Get Involved, including locally, statewide and of course with NIAAA." He continued saying, "Go to the NADC and take as many classes as you can!"

Tol went right into his #2 suggestion as he said "Keep on Learning … at every NADC Conference I've been to, I came away with something new!

It was my privilege to spend several years with Tol on the NIAAA Certification Committee where we got to listen to dozens of CMAA presentations that were presented orally. You need to find a way to us the tool of being a Life-Long Learner like my good friend, Tol Gropp!

Anne Campbell, CMAA and the Athletic Director at Grand Rapids High School in Minnesota says, "Reach out to other AD's in your area and Get Involved..." She continues with, "Once I got involved, I met so many incredible people!"

Anne reminds us about the importance to "Reach out because you're never alone!" Great Advice coming in at Tool #2.

Mike Ellson, CMAA and AD at Christ Presbyterian Academy in Nashville is a Master Administrator with an incredible national presence! Mike has already appeared on the list, and he returns here at #2 with his advice to "Get a Shoulder to cry on!" Mike goes on to explain that he means "…use the resources available including people and technology… and to find a Mentor!"

The thing that sticks out for me is that I've known Mike Ellson for quite a few years, and he is one of the most GIVING mentors we have in our organization. Find someone like Mike Ellson and get involved with a mentor or – if you are so called – Be a Mentor to someone else!

Peggy Seegers-Braun, CMAA and AD at Divine Savior Holy Angels High School in Milwaukie, Wisconsin checks in at #2 with the importance of "finding a seasoned Athletic Director" and also "getting involved with your state and the national (NIAAA) organization…" and "… when you make these connections, they allow you to so much more ... and you become more valuable!"

Peggy also shared the idea of how getting involved with great people "allows you to rise to a higher level by making connections and forming relationships." Some really great advice to put into your Athletic Director Toolbox!

Misty Buck out of Miami, Florida is a successful Author and Entrepreneur, and she has also written a book called The Athlete Mental Health Playbook. Misty shares this advice, "continue to learn ... go to workshops, read, and become more aware of how Mental Health affect health and performance."

Check out Misty's book and her website resources and add them to your Athletic Director Toolbox.

Mike Colby, CMAA makes another appearance in the Toolbox Top Four with his "tool" of "Getting Involved with a Mentor AD that you can call ... every day if needed..." as well as "getting involved with the NIAAA Leadership Training Program." He continued, "...these courses cover legal aspects, getting fields ready for a contest, or how to best service fans – these are all subjects covered in the LTI Courses."

Amber O'Malley is a CAA and the Assistant Athletic Director for the Community School of Naples, and she is also a member of the FIAAA Board of Directors. Amber's tool suggestions include "Get involved with your state association ... there is so much information and you will learn so much more that you imagined!"

Amber also shared, "... of course you grow through experience, but the information and knowledge you get from taking courses and participating in breakout sessions will prepare you for those experiences that you will have!" She finished by also sharing the importance of "Networking." Great advice from one of the FIAAA's rising stars!

Michael Harrison, CAA is the Director of Athletics at Orange Park High School near Jacksonville, Florida shows up here at Tool #2 with the importance to "Find a Mentor's phone number and don't be afraid to use it!"

Michael expanded on that thought with "you also need to get out of your comfort zone and call people that you don't know..." and keeping on the "Don't know" theme, he added "…when I first started as an AD – I didn't know what I didn't know, and I needed to reach out to people who knew more than I did…"

When you finally realize (for me it took way too long!) that you might not know everything, then you have a chance to get better! It Sounds like Michael figured that one out – make sure you do too!

Doug Killgore is a CMAA, and h is also a motivational speaker and high school athletics professional development specialist. Doug is also in the NIAAA Hall of Fame so it's a good idea to listen to his tool suggestions which include "Connect with the people around your state, and also get involved with the national organization."

Jon Payne, CMAA is the Athletic Director at Reading High School in Ohio and a long-time member of the NIAAA's Certification Committee. One of Jon's toolbox suggestions was "…just get involved – get involved at your local level, get involved at the state level, and find time to get involved at the national level."

He continued saying, "try to do it right away … I had to kinda fight to go to my first national conference … but I did it …" and "the relationships that you build and the information that you gain (by getting involved) will be priceless, and it is stuff that you will use the rest of your life!"

Once again, your humble author (if you say you're humble, are you?) put one of his toolbox tools here. I know for me, when I finally got involved with the FIAAA here in Florida, I believe that is when I begin to grow as an Athletic Director! I took one LTI course (taught by the great Dan Comeau, CMAA) and I was hooked! GET INVOLVED! You will be so glad that you did!

Julie Renner is a CAA and also an award-winning AD from Ohio recently was named as the Assistant Director for the Ohio Interscholastic Athletic Administrators Association. Julie also spent some time in the corporate world with Final Forms / AMP, so she has an idea of what works for Athletic Directors from both sides of the desk!

Julie's toolbox contributions include, "having Professional contacts by getting involved with your state association." She followed this up by saying "It's your Professional responsibility to get involved..." along with, "... there are so many people you can learn from."

Julie mentions, "I would have been lost as an AD (trying to manage a run through the state football playoffs) if I hadn't gotten involved in our state association."

Julie is so right! I like how she phrases it! Get Involved – it's Your Professional Responsibility

Don Bales, CMAA has already appeared on the AD toolbox countdown with good reason. Don is the NIAAA Director of Professional Development and oversees the National Committees including Certification, Coaches Education, and LTI as well as directing the State Coordinators meetings each year.

Here, Don shares his thoughts stating, "you need to find good Athletic Directors and learn from them!" He continued saying, "Connect with your state and national organizations as they provide the resources, workshops and courses you will need to gain the knowledge to do your job!"

Greg Warren, CMAA and Director of Athletics for the New Paltz School District in New York says, "Be involved in your Professional Organizations ... join your state association and join the NIAAA."

He continued saying, "Never Stop Learning, continue your education ..." and he added, "... we had an opportunity to be in the NIAAA Cohort (the first one) and even after 18 years, the Cohort was a great opportunity for us to continue to learn and stay fresh!"

Greg finished up by saying "getting involved, making those connections ... all you need to do is pick up the phone and talk to a fellow member ... there's someone out there waiting to help you!"

Ed Lockwood, CMAA from North Dakota is ANOTHER Hall of Famer that we got to visit with! Ed is a long time AD and Coach and former Executive Director for the North Dakota AD Association who now serves as the Assistant Program Director for NIAAA Certification.

Ed's toolbox also includes our #2 tool, stating "you need to know that you're not alone," adding "you are a part of a brotherhood and a sisterhood of tremendous people ... and the wonderful part of our organizations is that everyone wants YOU to be successful!"

Ed wrapped up with "… lean of them – don't be afraid to pick up the phone … and make sure you get involved with your state association and the NIAAA … and make sure you take the Leadership Training Courses…" Ed is without a doubt, a true Master Athletic Director! Make sure you have this tool in your toolbox!

Susan Noonan is the Athletic Director at the Ursuline School in Dallas, Texas and she was our 101st guest on the Educational AD Podcast! One of her toolbox tools was an encouragement to "Continue to Learn," saying "…get involved with the professional development programs that are available to you…"

Courtnay Windemaker, CAA and the Director of Athletics at Tenoric High School in Lakeland, Florida is back in the countdown with her tool suggestion "Don't be afraid to ask for help … you don't need to reinvent the wheel!"

Courtnay also shared "… we joke around but it's true, we beg borrow and steal good ideas from other athletic directors … and if they work at your school, that's great!"

The tool that Courtnay suggests is very true – Don't be afraid to ask another Athletic Director for help!

Suzanne Vick, CMAA is the Athletic Director at Curtis High School in University Place, Washington and she does a great job promoting her school's student athletes and coaches on social media!

One of Suzanne's contributions to the AD toolbox showed up here with "you have to ask questions." She followed up with "… you have to be willing to ask questions and not feel like you're dumb … and you also have to be willing to share new ideas when you get asked!"

I have gotten to know Suzanne this past year and she is a true visionary for her school and our profession! She is spot on with her tool suggestion here!

Our next contributor to the AD's Toolbox takes us up to the Great White North as we hear from Shannon Klassen who is the Executive Director of the CIAAA, the Canadian Interscholastic Athletic Administrators Association. Shannon's toolbox suggestion includes the importance of taking "Professional Development courses through CIAAA and NIAAA."

She added "… taking a crash course on what you need to know as and athletic director for your provincial (or state) association and for your school," and "getting all the tips, tricks, and ideas you need to survive … almost as a survival guide as an athletic director."

Shannon does a great job with her association – check it out at www.ciaaa.ca for some great ideas!

Cheryl Van Paris is up next, and she is the NIAAA Professional Development Manager working directly with the Certification Committee organizing all aspects of the CAA, RMSAA, and CMAA certifications.

One of Cheryl's tool suggestions appeared in this category as she shared the importance of "reaching out to your State Coordinator to find out what you don't know!" She added "I've found that Athletic Directors are much better at sharing Best Practices than principals (or coaches!) are."

Cheryl also suggested – and no surprise here – that "you need to start the Certification process" which she has a front row seat for as she receives the applications for CAA and CMAA in the National Office along with observing the CMAA Oral Presentations!

Reach out – contact and connect – with the folks at your state association!

We also got to hear from another member of the NIAAA's National Office during our interview with Justin Chapman who creates the content for the ADvantage blog.

Justin shared, "I was offered the opportunity to create and manage a blog and I also knew I wanted it to stand apart. The ADvantage is a place where I want to share personal thoughts and stories from ADs in a way that feels like you gained advice or perspective from a friend experiencing similar things you experience every day."

Justin also shared one of his toolbox tools with us, suggesting "visit the NIAAA website and find out where the athletic directors near you are…" and "find people to connect with." Justin also suggested "getting involved with committees along with taking classes, workshops, and webinars" which are all available online.

Some of our favorite interviews came during our three Student

Panels and our Texas Student Panel was no exception! Vivien Champ shared the tool of "you need to be a Life-Long Learner" as being important for everyone from student athletes to Athletic Directors! Its great to see and hear students preaching the benefits of lifelong learner – AD's, make sure this one is in your toolbox!

Our final contributor for this section is Cassidy Lichtman. Cassidy was one of our podcast guests who was not an Athletic Director, but she certainly knows her way around Athletics!

Cassidy was a two-time All American (and an Academic All American) while she was a member of the Stanford Volleyball Team, and she went on to play for the USA National Team as well as Professionally for a number of years before retiring as a player to help create P/ATH which is a non-profit which works within the sports world to develop skills around empathy and empowerment for athletes.

Cassidy's toolbox includes having "A willingness to learn," and she shared an anecdote from her time with the USA National Team and the head coach, Karch Kiraly, who is the unquestioned GOAT of volleyball. Cassidy says, "the first day of practice, Karch came into the gym and said – Rule #1 is We ALL are Learners…" which was "pretty incredible because everyone in that gym was among the best in the world…" and Coach Kiraly's point was, "We are all going to learn to get Better!"

Great advice from an impressive source! Be a Life-Long Learner! Get Better!

Other Athletic Directors we interviewed on the podcast who shared this particular tool included –

Tammie Talley, CAA – Florida (Professional Development)

Tara Osbourne, CAA – Alabama (Get Involved)

Pam Lancaster, CMAA – Florida (Ask for Help)

Steve Throne, CMAA – Nebraska (Have a Growth Mindset)

Russell Wambles, CMAA – Florida (Professional Development)

Kandice Mitchell, CMAA – Georgia (Professional Development)

Shelton Crews of FACA – Florida (Get Involved

Stephanie Blackwell, CMAA – Oklahoma (Get Involved)

Jay Radar, CAA – Florida (Get Involved)

Kate Williams, CAA – Oregon (Get Involved)

Marcus Gabriel, CAA – Florida (Ask for Help)

Chris Fore, CAA – California (Get Involved)

Mary Walker – Florida (Get Involved)

Brad Montgomery, CAA – Florida (Professional Development)

Meg Seng, CMAA – Michigan (Get Involved)

Roger Mayo, CMAA – Florida (Get Involved)

Nicole Norris, CAA – Michigan (Get Involved)

Lorna Wolfkill, CAA – Florida (Ask for Help)

Nate Larsen, CMAA – Nebraska (Life-long learner)

Lyle Livingood, CAA – Florida (Ask for Help)

Dr. Mekia Troy, CAA – Georgia (Use all of your resources)

Robert Blackman – Washington (Ask for Help)

Justin Chapman, NIAAA – Indiana (Webinars/IAA Magazine)

Rob Seymour, CMAA – Indiana (Ask for Help)


And now …. Drum roll …. Here is the #1 Tool (most frequently mentioned) as suggested by our podcast interviews!

# CHAPTER 20

Tool # 1 – **Network and Get a Mentor!**

The Toolbox Top Twenty most frequently suggested Tool for the Athletic Director's Toolbox was Networking with other AD's along with Find a Mentor AD.

On its own, this tool was mentioned by 13% of our Athletic Directors and as mentioned earlier - Combined with the #2 tool most frequently recommended tool – Get Involved – they both made up **25%** of all the tools that were suggested!

The 63 responses for this tool were fairly evenly distributed between **Mentor** vs **Network**, and they were also balanced evenly between Men and Women.

In the interviews, CMAA's gave Mentoring / Networking the nod more frequently than CAA's, but those Athletic Directors without a CAA or CMAA also mentioned the value of Networking and Mentoring almost 20 times!

This is a good time to remind you that every one of our State Associations – as well as the NIAAA – has a mentoring coordinator and an AD Mentoring program to serve its members. Reach out today, and either ask for a mentor or if you are ready, BECOME a Mentor for another Athletic Director! Use the NIAA's Athletic Director Network and the NIAAA Portal to grow and to help our Profession grow!

Now let's look at the Athletic Directors who had the #1 Tool in their Toolbox …

Pam Lancaster, CMAA and Athletic Director at Auburndale High School in Florida leads off with her suggestion to "Network with other AD's and feel free to borrow good ideas!"

She continues, saying "… Its ok to use someone else's ideas – even though I'm entering my 20th year, I still use any great idea that I think will fit at my school," and "… it might be on how to do paperwork, or organize something, or help one of your programs … but it's important to know that it's OK to use a great idea!"

Pam is a real pro, and a new idea she really uses well is making Tik Tok videos of her students, her teams, and even herself at a game or a practice! Try this idea at your school and see if it is a good fit!

Kandice Mitchell is not just a CMAA and an award-winning Athletic Director for the Atlanta Public School system, but she has an incredible background as a former D-I and International athlete and until a recent injury, STILL competed in the Women's National Football Conference as a player!

Kandice shares her toolbox tool with this – "Get connected with a veteran AD … someone you can call with your questions." She added how "… its important to Network because there are so many of us – not just in the state where you are but across the nation and even international!"

Kandice also said, "Find out what is going on out there at other schools because it will not only make you a better person but also a better Athletic Director!"

Tyrone McGriff, CAA and the AD at the Florida State University School in Tallahassee, shared his unique perspective of growing up in an Educational and Athletic (Professional Football) family.

Tyrone's tools included "… get registered as a member of the NIAAA." He also shared how a certain Athletic Director encouraged him, saying "… you don't realize how that one conversation you had with me where you told me to (get involved with FIAAA / NIAA) … you couldn't have given me anything more useful than what you gave me … the opportunity to learn." Thank You Tyrone, for those kind words!

You never know how your words are going to impact someone, but you can always know it's a good thing to get involved!

Dixie Wescott is another CMAA who has a stellar coaching

career at both the high school and the college level before moving on to a career as an Athletic Director. Dixie is currently the Program Director for the William Woods University Online Masters Program in Athletic Administration, so she is connected to new and veteran AD's.

Her tool suggestion for this category was to "Network – it's very important to reach out to veteran AD's and Administrators." She felt is was "… take ideas and try them out at your building."

Like many other podcast guests, Dixie shared "don't try to reinvent the wheel … there are so many AD's out there that are willing to help … seek them out!"

Ron Allan, Lecanto High School (Florida) and FIAAA Board of Directors makes another appearance on the list with the following tool – "Bottom line, get a mentor!' and he added "… get somebody who has experience and knows how to do things, and get them on speed-dial!"

Ron also suggested "you might think you know things, but you don't know…" and "my mentors helped me get involved in FIAAA and NIAAA when I first was offered the job!" As Ron says – Bottom Line … Get a Mentor!

Ron was also one of only Five Athletic Directors, whose own toolbox suggestions all ended up in the Top Three Categories! Remember, ALL of the tools are valuable – these just happened to be mentioned more frequently!

Scott Drabczyk, CAA is the very successful AD at Father Lopez Catholic in Daytona Beach, Florida. Scott's toolbox suggestions included this - "The first thing I'm going to tell them is they need to get a Mentor, whether it's through the FIAAA or just someone in your building, you have to have someone you can lean on!"

Scott felt very strongly about "you need to have someone you can go to with questions or just to vent … you can't do this job on your own," and he added "… you may have won 20 state titles as a coach, but as soon as you're on the other side of that desk, your world changes completely and you're going to need someone to be by your side!"

Tol Gropp, CMAA from Timberline High School in Boise shared the tool of "… finding a bigger group of AD's to help you understand what you're doing!" Tol said, "When I started out, that first year was tough … and now I'm in year 15, and its tougher – the expectations have gone up – and you need that network of Athletic Directors that you can go to."

Stephanie Blackwell, CMAA is a state and national award-winning AD who shared her knowledge and passion for athletics on the podcast! She is also a member of the NIAAA Certification Committee which puts her on the cutting edge of developments in certification and Leadership Training.

Stephanie's toolbox suggestion for this category was to "Find that Mentor that will help you know what is going on;' which will help you be organized (tool #3) and also help you get involved (tool #2) with your state organization.

Stephanie was another one of the Five Athletic Directors whose three Tool Suggestions ended up in the Top Three!

Dr. Lisa Langston, CMAA and current NIAAA President also makes another appearance in the countdown with this tool! Dr. Langston shares that "you really need to get a mentor," saying "If you don't know something ask questions."

She also said, "If there is someone in the area you admire, or even someone you haven't met, reach out to them and if you have to make a big decision, ask them what they think … let them know what you're thinking about doing."

Once again, find that mentor who can help you become a better Athletic Director!

Casey Thiele, CAA and the Athletic Director at Pensacola High School in the NW corner of Florida offered this tool, saying "… I have to have a list of people that I can call when I need to solve a problem."

Casey added to this thought, "We have a great county AD who has helped mentor me so I can call him along with some other building Ads if I need to!"

Footnote - as of this writing, Casey is the new county AD as the previous AD – Roger Mayo, who is also in this countdown - has retired! I can easily see Casey becoming the same kind of great mentor that Roger was!

Shelton Crews, who is the Executive Director of the Florida Athletic Coaches Association, has already appeared in the toolbox countdown and he's back again with our most popular tool!

Shelton suggests that "a new AD needs to start by creating a Network, and you do that by attending the FACA Clinics and the FIAAA Conference..." adding "those organizations are where you will help create your support group and the conversations you have will be invaluable!"

Jay Radar, CAA is another Hall of Fame AD who participated in our countdown. Jay helps organize our FIAAA Newsletter and his toolbox contribution appears here in the #1 Category.

Jay quotes the old saying, "No Man is an Island" and he adds to it with "...you need to have that Rolodex ... have the name of the person who talked you into becoming an AD or an AD who you admire and maybe would like to model yourself after..."

Jay's point is, "You need to have someone that you can talk to, and if you don't have someone in mind, contact your FIAAA board member (or your state association) ... and we will take care of you!"

Steve Throne is a CMAA from Nebraska and one of the catalysts for the Podcast to expand beyond Florida and I am very grateful for his encouragement!

Steve's toolbox suggestion included "Find people who are doing things on a high level, and then network with them!" He added "when I was first starting out, I'd call 5 or 6 AD's and ask them the same question ... I'll network with anybody because I know there are always people who are doing things better than me, and that's how I get better!"

Great stuff Steve! It's easy to see why your program is so good!

Stacey Segal, CMAA and Assistant Director of Athletics for the Dallas Independent School District shows up in our #1 tool category with her suggestion to "Find a Mentor - both personal and professional... someone you can bounce ideas off of."

She also shared "In this profession, we don't steal, but we do share..." adding, "... I share your quotes pretty much on a daily basis," referring to the multitude of quotes and phrases that I post on social media! I really appreciate the shout out, Stacey, but I think you and your program are the real stars!

Lynn Flint, CAA is the Athletic Director at Haddam Killingworth School in Connecticut, and her toolbox suggestion is "Create a strong network, right off the bat, connecting with those people around you."

Lynn also shared the importance of "when you're connected to those people, they will come with you wherever you go, even if it's just one or even two AD's in your town or your area."

I had the pleasure of presenting with Lynn a couple of years ago at the NADC and it's been great to watch her grow her program. I encourage you to connect with Lynn and add her to your network!

Chris Fore, CAA is another one of our "Fantastic Five" podcast guests who had all 3 of their tools make our Countdown's Top 3. Chris is a former Coach and AD who is now a very successful Principal, and he also runs a very successful consulting program called EightLaces.com (check it out!)

It is no surprise he shows up here with his tool of "having a mentor, someone that you can pick up the phone and call them..."

Chris added he's staring a Coaches Mentoring program out in his state, and he added, "Getting a mentor for Coaches, Head Coaches, and Athletic Directors is something I really believe in!"

Great stuff, Chris! And make sure you check out Chris's website too!

Michael Harrison, CAA and Athletic Director at Orange Park High School in Jacksonville, Florida is also a member of our Fantastic Five Club, and his toolbox suggestion is "Find a Mentor and call them," adding "I had a mentor who I called a lot, but I also got out of my comfort zone and called some other AD's."

Michael also mentioned that "reaching out to those guys has allowed me to grow and get better ..." and it will do the same for you. Find a Mentor and let them help you get better!

Jonathan Bukva, CMAA and Director of Athletics at Virginia's Ronald Reagan Middle School is the final member of our Fantastic Five – all 3 of Jonathan's Toolbox suggestions ended up in our Toolbox Top 3.

Jonathan had a new assistant AD this year who happened to be a woman, and he not only offered to be her "Mentor" but Jonathan also encouraged her to get involved with Jen Brooks' Global

Community of Women in High School Sports website which as I've already mentioned, is a GREAT resource for an AD. Jonathan also gave a shout out to the NIAAA Portal as a great networking resource, which is where he and I first "networked!" Check it out and make your own network work for you!

Mary Walker, the Athletic Director at Fernandina Beach High on Florida's Amelia Island also appears at Tool # 1 with ... "reach out to other athletic directors and get advice... ask them what they are doing ... socialize with them at FHSAA and FIAAA meetings ... and have a sounding board you can go to."

Mary also shared "It's not a sign of weakness to ask for help or advice ... and at some point, people are going to start calling on you for your opinion, and that feels good!"

Great advice from a veteran Athletic Director! Reach out!

Brad Montgomery, CAA of Seabreeze High School in Ormond Beach, Florida shows up in the #1 Tool Category with his tool which was "... I'm going to give that new AD my phone number, because they're going to need it – they're going to need my experience."

Brad added this nugget as their future mentor, saying "learn as much as you can and be willing to work with everyone!" Brad has done a great job at his school, and he also does a great job as the FIAAA District Director for his area. Thanks for all you do!

Jake von Scherrer (your humble author) also contributed to this category when he was interviewed by Dr. Tim Baghurst of the Florida State University Coaching School, saying "seek out the very best people with experience ... maybe the best teacher ... and ask what you do in your classroom, how do you motivate people...?"

The point I was making is you need to find a mentor(s) to help you become the very best version of you! Find a mentor!

It was my honor to follow the great Roger Mayo as the President of the FIAAA and Roger shows up here on the toolbox top twenty! Roger is a CMAA and the longtime Escambia County AD in Pensacola, Florida.

Roger shares his toolbox suggestion with "you need to learn to be yourself, but you also need to get a mentor and establish your network ... reach out to those who can help you!"

I know Roger was one of those AD's who was on my "go to" list when I had a question. Establish your network and get a mentor!

Meg Seng, CMAA and Athletic Director at Michigan's Greenhills School and a team-mate of mine on the NIAAA National Certification Committee. She also founded the Academy for Sport Leadership – check it out at www.sportleadership.net
Meg's toolbox tools included "Don't walk alone – there are so many good people out there, including your coaching staff, so if you support your staff, they will support you!" Meg finished off this idea with "Find a Mentor!" Without a doubt, Meg Seng is on of our profession's very best!

During my time in Tallahassee, Florida I've gotten to know Lorna Wolfkill, CAA who is the AD at Community Christian School and she does a great job of promoting her teams and her programs!
Lorna contributes to the Toolbox tool of Networking with "Get to know other AD's, including those in your area at similar schools and those who are at bigger schools or schools across the county."
Lorna also added this thought, which she said came from one of my coaches at the Maclay School who she counts as a mentor, "...don't worry, I've already done everything wrong at least once! It happens, and it will be ok!" That is a great example of mentoring!

Nicole Norris, CAA who is the AD at East Lansing High School in East Lansing, Michigan shows up here with her toolbox suggestion of "... the number one thing is to pick up the phone and contact a mentor!"
Nicole also says, "It took me a couple of years to figure this out ..." and encourages everyone to not wait to do this! I have got to know Nicole a little bit this past year and I can tell you she is really a quality Athletic Director!

Nate Larsen, CMAA and Assistant Principal/Athletic Director at Logan View Jr/Sr. HS in Hooper, Nebraska also had Networking on his list of Tools saying "Creating a Network, which for me has come through the NIAAA portal and the Nebraska AD Association..."
Nate continued, "get to know your peers, lean on them for advice, there is a wealth of resources out there." He gave another

shout out for the NIAAA Portal saying, "without the NIAAA Portal, I don't know if I would have met you!" I don't know how important that was (connecting with me!) but I can tell you Nate is right about using the NIAAA Portal to connect and network! If you are not already using it, please add it to your toolbox!

Deb Margolis is the Athletic Director at the TERRA School which is The Environmental Research Institute in South Florida. Deb is a long time Florida AD who previously built Coral Reef High School. into a powerhouse before leaving to take over the program at TERRA.

Deb's Athletic Director Toolbox Tools included finding a mentor, saying "Find a Mentor – maybe an Athletic Director or an Administrator that has been through what you're going to go through ... someone you can trust and rely on and reach out to any time night or day!"

Our next AD on the toolbox countdown is my old high school teammate Robert Blackman, who is now the Athletic Director at Mark Morris High School in Longview, Washington.

Robert shares his tool suggestion with something that his District does for new AD's saying "... in the email we send out to all new AD's it says –

"As part of OUR culture... we do work together!"

Robert went on saying, "we want them to know you are not alone, and that there are other Athletic Directors out there to help you ... people who have done it before – people who will lend you a hand," and ending with "don't try to do it by yourself – you are part of a team!"

What a great tool for new (and old!) Athletic Directors! Thanks, Robert, for sharing this one!

Rob Seymour, CMAA is the Director of Athletics at Fishers High School in Indiana, and his unique toolbox idea of "PQR – Pretty Quick Return" shows up again here is the #1 Category.

Rob says, and one of his "P" tools, to be "Professional, and by that, I (Rob) mean get out there and Network with other Athletic Directors..." and then he adds his "Q" meaning "ask Questions of other AD's about your own procedures – ask if they need to be modified." Rob was one of those AD's, and there were a few, who managed to sneak in for than 3 tools but that is OK! I appreciate the effort to add to the Athletic Directors Toolbox!

One of the things I appreciate most about doing the **Educational AD Podcast** is the opportunity to make new friends and also connect with "old friends" that I do not get to see as often! One of those old friends is Marc "Hutch" Hunter, CMAA who is the Executive Director of the UIAAA and a longtime Utah coach and AD.

Marc also has his own podcast – modeled after another "very successful podcast" called the UIAAA Connection which I encourage you to check out! Mark contributed to the Toolbox Top Twenty with his suggestion to "You need to network and get involved with your state association..."

Marc went on saying "you need to begin your network, because when I started, I just didn't know anyone ... and now I can just pick up the phone and talk to someone who has already gone through just about everything I will ever go through ..."

One more thing about Hutch - I am going to put in a plug for his great book, Plateau. I have read it and it's really a great story with great characters! I encourage you to check it out on Amazon!

Kari Avila, CAA is the Athletic Director at Salome High School in Arizona, and her #1 Toolbox suggestion was "Network!" Kari shared that when she first got the job, "I got a phone message from some guy and I asked my principal – who is this – and he said, THAT is your guy ... when he calls, you answer!" That guy was her mentor!

Kari added, "Have that list of people you can call ... have your long list but also have that short list of people you can call on a Sunday night at ten o'clock at night and they will answer!"

Another AD offering the valuable tool of creating your Network!

Suzanne Vick, CMAA and the AD at Curtis High School in Washington appeared with the #2 tool of "asking for help," and she also suggested the #1 tool with, "When you get the job, you have to find your go to person..."

Suzanne followed this up with, "You've got to find that one person that you can talk to and seek advice from," adding "being an AD is ... so scattered, and you're not going to have all of the answers!" She continued with "... my mentor helped me understand eligibility and understand the different situations that we deal with!" Suzanne Vick is truly on point suggesting this tool!

I first met Kelly Blount when we both served as members our state's FHSAA Section I Appeals Committee, and I immediately saw he knew what he was talking about! Kelly is the AD at Atlantic Coast High School in Jacksonville, Florida and his suggestion of "Networking" also appears here.

Kelly says, "use other Athletic Directors as resources," along with "… most of us are using stuff or stealing stuff like you should when you find a better way of doing things!"

Kelly also shared, "There are a handful of AD's that I call every day and we share things back and forth …" adding, "you just can't store everything up in your head and you can't get to your desk all the time, so use the resource of other Athletic Directors!"

Dr. Mekia Troy, CAA who does a great job as the Athletic Director at Creekside H.S. in Douglasville, Georgia also suggested the #1 tool saying, "get the contact info of other AD's, maybe some that are a little more seasoned, so you can reach out get other perspectives, to get advice … it doesn't hurt to get another opinion to allow you to see other sides of an issue."

Dr. Troy is someone that I would encourage any Athletic Director to reach out and add to their mentoring network!

Our final contributor to the Category #1 Tool is Shea Collins, CAA who serves as the Activities/Athletic Director at Midlothian High School in Virginia.

Shea's suggestion for this tool started out with, "Number one, I'm going to give them a Mentor Card, but they are going to fill out the names that will go on it!" Shea also mentioned that "none of us got to where we are overnight…" and she spoke glowingly about the mentors she has had during her career.

Since this "Tool" was the most popular, or frequently mentioned tool, in our countdown - we obviously we had a lot of Athletic Directors who also listed "Networking" or "Get a Mentor" as one of their AD toolbox tools so, here are the other Athletic Directors who had this tool in their Athletic Director Toolbox –

John Sgromolo, CAA – Florida (Mentor)

Kiesha Brown, CMAA – Georgia (Seek out the previous AD)

Steve McHale, CAA – Florida (Network)

Allison Fondale, CMAA – Maryland (Network)

Kelly Fish, CMAA – Tennessee (Network)

Mike Ostrowski – Florida (Network)

Anne Campbell, CMAA – Minnesota (Network)

Dr. Danielle LaPoint – Florida (Mentor)

Mike Ellson, CMAA – Tennessee (Mentor)

Mike Colby, CMAA – Florida (Mentor)

Lisa Gingras, CMAA – New Hampshire (Mentor)

Monica Maxwell, CMAA – Indiana (Mentor)

Doug Killgore, CMAA – Arkansas (Network)

Jon Payne, CMAA – Ohio (Network)

Tim Leeseburg, CAA – Florida (Mentor)

Don Bales, CMAA – Indiana (Mentor)

Greg Warren, CMAA – New York (Network)

Shay Steele, Ohio – (Network)

Courtnay Windemaker, CAA – Florida (Network)

Darlene Bible, CMAA – California (Network)

Drew Hanson – Canada (CIAAA Network)

Lacey London, CAA – Washington (Network)

Justin Chapman, NIAA Office – Indiana (Network)

Michelle Noeth, CAA – California (Network)

Gary Stevens, CMAA – Maine (Mentor)

Jerri Kelly, CAA – Florida (Mentor)

Moe Orr – California (Mentor)

Shannon Klassen – Canada (Network)

Stevi Balsamo, CAA – California (Network)

Cheryl Van Paris, NIAA Office – Indiana (Mentor)


And there you have it! Can I say WOW? I'm going to say it – WOW!

The Educational AD Podcast's **Athletic Director Toolbox.**

A total of 155 Interviews (152 Athletic Directors and Professionals, plus we included our 3 Student Panels) where we heard a grand total of 475 Toolbox Suggestions.

I hope you have found it to be interesting, and maybe just a little bit entertaining, but my greatest hope is that you have found it informative and that it becomes a resource for you and other AD's.

So many of our contributors offered this comment during our chats, which I also have said many times …

***"If only I had all of this when I was first starting out …"***

I really wish I could have had all of these "Tools" as a young teacher and coach even before I first became an AD and then, once I was handed these tools, I could have been smart enough to USE them!

Now that you have these tools in your Athletic Director Toolbox, I again hope that you find the right tools for you, and that you also use them to help your programs become the very best that they (and you!) can be!

I will close with one of my favorite phrases. I cannot recall the first time I heard it or who it should be attributed to, as it is not my creation, but I have taken it wherever I have gone and used it frequently for at least the past 20+ years!

The coaches I have worked with during that time also know it well, and – as their Athletic Director – I was blessed to have them embrace it with their team and our program. I truly believe in the idea that this message, and I encourage you to use the tools in the Toolbox Top Twenty to help make this theme a truism when people take a look at your school and your program –

*"Everything you see at your school is either <u>Coached</u>, or it is <u>Allowed</u> ... Which one is it for you?"*

Make sure everything you (and others) SEE at your school is Coached the way it should be! Use the tools we have been given to make your school the very best it can be!

# AFTERWORD

This project has an interesting history, starting with my childhood and playing games in the backyard, the street, and so many fields and playgrounds (who had a gym?) in my neighborhood.

Fast forward to middle school, high school, and then competing (playing) in college before the first 40 years of my coaching and AD career, before I got inspired to start a podcast where the Athletic Director's Toolbox was born.

It has been so great to hear the incredible stories that our first 150+ guests have shared, and I am so grateful that everyone has been so giving of their time and their knowledge! To the real experts of our profession, I offer a very humble and a very sincere, "Thank You!"

Here they are, in the order that their episode was recorded –

**Volume 1:**
1   Rocky Gillis, CAA – Broward Co. Athletic Association (Florida)
2   Tammie Talley, CAA – Duval Co. Schools (Florida)
3   Dan Talbot, CMAA – Polk Co. Schools (Florida)
4   Pam Lancaster, CMAA – Auburndale High School AD (Florida)
5   Steve Ripley, CMAA – FIAAA Board of Directors (Florida)
6   Jay Getty, CAA – Hagerty High School (Florida)
7   John Sgromolo, CAA – Clay Co. AD (Florida)
8   Jessica Upchurch, CAA – Sebastian River High School (Florida)
9   Russell Wambles, CMAA – FIAAA Board of Directors (Florida)
10 Andy Warner – Warner Soccer / Maclay School (Florida)
11 Kandice Mitchell, CMAA – Atlanta Public Schools (Georgia)
12 Ashton Washington – Texas Tech Football (Texas)
13 Alison Posey – WTXL/ABC 27 Reporter (Florida)
14 Tyrone McGriff, CAA – Florida State University School (Florida)
15 Kiesha Brown, CMAA – The Galloway School (Georgia)
16 Wayne Stofsly – The David Posnack School (Florida)
17 Jennifer Brooks, CMAA – Ursuline School St. Loius (Missouri)
18 Ernest Robertson, Jr. CMAA – Palmer Trinity School (Florida)
19 Dixie Wescott, CMAA – William Woods University (Missouri)
20 Steve McHale, CAA – Dr. Phillips High School (Florida)

21 Rebecca Moe – University Prep (Washington)
22 Ron Allan – Lecanto High School (Florida)
23 Stephanie Blackwell, CMAA – Bixby High School (Oklahoma)
24 Peter Shambo, CMAA – Penfield School District (New York)
25 Holly Farnese, CMAA – Pennsylvania AD Association
26 Scott Drabczyk, CAA – Father Lopez Catholic School (Florida)
27 Allision Fondale, CMAA – St. Mary's High School (Maryland)
28 Tol Gropp, CMAA – Timberline High School (Idaho)
29 Dr. Lisa Langston, CMAA – Ft. Worth School District (Texas)
30 Dr. Chris Hobbs, CMAA – The King's Academy (Florida)
31 Tara Osborne, CAA – Prattville Christian Academy (Alabama)
32 Casey Thiele, CAA – Pensacola High School (Florida)
33 Kelly Fish, CMAA – Currey Ingram Academy (Tennessee)
34 Shelton Crews – Florida Athltic Coaches Association
35 Kippie Crouch, CAA – Out of Door Academy (Florida)
36 Mike Ostrowski, CAA – North Broward Prep (Florida)
37 Amanda Waters, CAA – St. Andrews School (Georgia)
38 Jay Radar, CAA – FIAAA Board of Directos (Florida)
39 Anne Campbell, CMAA – Grand Rapids H.S. (Minnesota)
40 Joey Struwe, CMAA – Lincoln High School (South Dakota)
41 Dr. Danielle LaPoint – Manatee High Schoo (Florida)
42 Mike Ellson, CMAA – Christ Presbyterian Acad. (Tennesee)
43 Becky Moran, CMAA – Round Lake High School (Illinois)
44 Dan Comeau, CMAA – FIAAA Board of Directors) Florida
45 Carol Dozibrin, CMAA – New Hampshire AD Association
46 Mark Lee, CAA – Hernando High School (Florida)
47 Deb Savino, CMAA – Ransom Everglades School (Florida)
48 Rich Barton, CMAA – Richfield High School (Utah)
49 Caterine Tanco-Ong – Brent International School (Phillipines)
50 Nathan Stanley, CAA – Lakeridge High School (Oregon)
51 Peggy Seeger-Braun, CMAA – Divine Savior Holy Angels (Wisc.)
52 Steve Throne, CMAA – Millard South High School (Nebraska)
53 Steri Stice, CMAA – NIAAA Certification Director (Texas)
54 Dan Schuster, CMAA – NFHS Dir. of Learning (Indiana)
55 Stacey Segal, CMAA – Dallas Independent School Dist. (Texas)
56 Dr. Kaleb Stoppel, CMAA – Olathe East High School (Kansas)
57 Misty Buck – Author, Lecturer, Mental Health Coach (Florida)
58 Mike Colby, CMAA – FIAAA Board of Directors (Florida)

59 Lynne Flint, CAA – Haddam Killingworth School (Connecticut)
60 Marcus Gabriel, CAA – American High School (Florida)
61 Cheryl Shivel – Astronaut High School (Florida)
62 Charlie Marello, Principal – Niceville High School (Florida)
63 Amber O'Malley, CAA – Community School of Naples (Florida)
64 Chris Fore, CAA – Palmdale Aerospace Academy (California)
65 Pam Cawley, CAA – Foundation Christian Academy (Florida)
66 Michael Harrison, CAA – Orange Park High School (Florida)
67 Lisa Gingras, CMAA – Nashua High School (New Hampshire)
68 Jonathan Bukva, CMAA –Ronald Regan Middle School (Virginia)
69 Monica Maxwell, CMAA – East Central Chicago H.S. (Indiana)
70 Doug Killgore, CMAA – NIAAA Hall of Fame (Arkansas)
71 Mary Walker – Fernandina Beach High School (Florida)
72 Dr. Dustin Smith, CMAA – Greenwood High School (Arkansas)
73 Anne Julian, CAA Holy Cross High School (Kentucky)
74 Jason Frey, CAA – Pompano Beach High School (Florida)
75 Kate Williams – Catlin Gable School (Oregon)
76 Jamie Sheetz, CMAA – Park City High School (Utah)
77 Kristin Peeples, CAA – Nature Coast Technical (Florida)
78 Brad Montgomery, CAA – Seasbreeze High School (Florida)
79 Ann Stewert, CAA – Los Alamos Highs School (New Mexico)
80 Jon Payne, CMAA – Reading High School (Ohio)
81 Marion House, CAA – Nixa High School (Missouri)
82 Josh Blumenthal – St. Andrews Episcopal School (Texas)
83 Tim Leeseburg, CAA – Plant City High School (Florida)
84 Dr. David Kelly, CAA – Univeristy of Cinncinati (Ohio)
85 Nicole Ebsen, CAA – Morton High School (Illinois)
86a Jake von Scherrer, CMAA – The Maclay School (Florida)
86b Roger Mayo, CMAA – Escambia Co. Schools (Florida)
87 Julie Renner, CAA – Ohio Interscholastic Ath. Dir. Assoc.
88 Rob Paschall – Assr Head Football Coach, Creekviw HS (Texas)
89 Meg Seng, CMAA – Greenhills School (Michigan)
90 Don Bales, CMAA – NIAAA Profession Dev. Coord. (Indiana)
91 Lorna Wolfkill – Community Christian School (Florida)
92 Greg Warren, CMAA – New Paltz Schools (New York)
93 Sally Ann Reis – CEO of PlayyOn sports platform (California)
94 Quante Speight, CAA – Mallard Creek H.S. (North Carolina)
95 Shay Steele – Walnut Hills High School (Ohio)

96 Ed Lockwood, CMAA – NIAAA Program Coor. (North Dakota)
97 Nicole Norris, CAA – East Lansing High School (Michigan)
98 Mike McGurk, CMAA – Summit High School (Missouri)
99 Jay Hammes, CMAA – SafeSportsZone Founder (Wisconsin)
100 Don Baker, CAA and Josh Matthews, CMAA – Hangin With the AD Podcast hosts (Georgia)

## Volume 2:

1  Susan Noonan – Ursuline School of Dallas (Texas)
2  Nate Larsen, CMAA – Logan View Jr./Sr. High (Nebraska
3  Deb Margolis – The TERRA School (Florida)
4  Lyle Livingood, CAA – West Port High School (Florida)
5  Jackie Randall, CAA – Elk Grove High School (Illinois)
6  Josh Wilson – Publisher FloridaHSFootball.com (Florida)
7  Jennifer Doede, RAA – Joliet Central High School (Illinois)
8  Akelah Reeves & Sam Magliore – Student Panel #1 (Florida)
9  Courtnay Windemake, CAA – Tenoroc High School (Florida)
10 Robert Blackman – Mark Morris High School (Washington)
11a Darlend Bible, CMAA – Harvard-Westlake School (California)
11b Flynn Baliton, Patrick Hayburn, Hope Davis – Student Panel 2
12  Drew Hanson – Canadian Interscholatic Athletic Admin. Assoc.
13  Lacey London, CAA – Holy Names Academy (Washington)
14  Rob Seymour, CMAA – Fishers High School (Indiana)
15 Dr. Keisha Rowles, CAA – Rockdale Co. Schools (Georgia)
16  John Beau Drake – Asst. Principal Heritage H.S.(North Carolina)
17 Michelle Noeth, CAA – Los Altos High Schoo (California)
18 Marc "Hutch" Hunter – Exec. Director of the UIAAA (Utah)
19 Kari Avila, CAA – Salome High School (Arizona)
20 Gary Stevens, CMAA – Thorton Academy (Maine)
21 Suzanne Vick, CMAA – Curtis High School (Washington)
22 Antony Fisher, CMAA – Minneapolis Public Schools (Minnesota)
23 Jerri Kelly, CAA – Lake Brantley High School (Florida)
24 Brian Nolan, CAA – Charlotte High School (Florida)
25 Teresa Gunter – Leon High School (Florida)
26 Moe Orr – The High School Narrative (California)
27 Shanon Klassen - Canadian Interscholatic Athletic Admin. Assoc.
28 Mark Rosenbalm, CMAA – Collier Co. Schools (Florida)
29 Melanie Redd – Melanie Redd Performance Training (Ohio)
30 David Marlow, CMAA – Mnt. Mansfield Union H.S. (Vermont)

31 Kelly Blount, CAA – Atlantic Coast High School (Florida)
32 Teg Cosgriff, CMAA – Westbrook Public Schools (Connecticut)
33 Emily Barkley, CMAA – Union Public Schools (Oklahoma)
34 Bob Bruglio, CAA – Port Charlotte High School (Florida)
35 Dr. Mekia Troy, CAA – Creekside High School (Georgia)
36 Ken Edwards, CMAA – Jamestown High School (Virginia)
37 Annette Scogin, CMAA – NIAAA Past President (Arkansas)
38 Doug Stephens – Senior Pastor LivetheLife (Florida)
39 Stevi Balsamo, CAA – Millennium High School (California)
40 Jim Harris, CMAA – T.C. Williams High School (Virginia)
41 Cheryl Van Paris – NIAAA Certification Prog. Manager (Indiana)
42 Dr. Greg Dale – Duke University Leadership (North Carolina)
43 Laura Zamora – City Year in Miami (Florida)
44 Justin Chapman – NIAAA Copywirtier (Indiana)
45 Shea Collins, CAA – Midlothian High School (Virginia)
46 Josh Scott, CMAA – Springfield Co. School District (Missoui)
47a Cassidy Lichtman – Director of P/ATH (California)
47b Ben Center, Vivien Champ, Mark Greenburg: Student Panel #3
48 Chris Hall, CMAA – Discovery High School (Georgia)
49 Lisa McCullough, CMAA – The Bush School (Washington)
50 Darryl Nance, CMAA – Greenville Co. Schools (South Carolina)

Moving forward, The Educational AD Podcast continues to record episodes where we allow Athletic Directors to 1.) Share their story, 2.) Brag a little bit on their school, and 3.) Offer some Best Practices for AD's. The formula seems to work so as people keep listening, we will continue to record them!

For those Athletic Directors whose interview came after the first 150 episodes, your Toolbox Tools will be presented in the 2nd Edition of **The Athletic Director's Toolbox** which will be published in the summer of 2022. Until then, I hope everyone will continue to listen to The Educational AD Podcast which can be heard on the following platforms –

**Anchor**
https://anchor.fm/educational-ad-podcast

**Breaker**
https://www.breaker.audio/educational-ad-podcast

**Google Podcasts**
https://www.google.com/podcasts?feed=aHR0cHM6Ly9hbm
Nob3IuZm0vcy8yNzEyZGZmMC9wb2RjYXN0L3Jzcw==

**Apple Podcasts**
https://podcasts.apple.com/us/podcast/educational-ad-podcast/id1519847584?uo=4

**Overcast**
https://overcast.fm/itunes1519847584/educational-ad-podcast

**Pocket Casts**
https://pca.st/wq21e91j

**RadioPublic**
https://radiopublic.com/educational-ad-podcast-69AdlQ

**Spotify**
https://open.spotify.com/show/6qUnXSZKJCYd3or9IMsIJE

Also, the Zoom recordings of our interviews are always being uploaded to the Educational AD Podcast YouTube Channel.

I hope the **Athletic Director's Toolbox** has been a nice addition to your professional library. If you have suggestions or you would like to be a guest on the podcast, please feel free to reach out to me! My email is jakestouchdown@gmail.com

Thanks, and as I like to say, "Keep Coaching Those Coaches!" All the Best in your adventures as an Educational Athletic Director.

Jake von Scherrer – June, 2021

# ABOUT THE AUTHOR

Jake von Scherrer is a career Educator and a Certified Master Athletic Administrator with 41 years of success as a teacher, a Head Coach, and as an AD. Recently retired as the Director of Athletic Enrichment at The Maclay School, an independent college prep school in Tallahassee, Florida, Jake also served as the 2020-21 President of the Florida Interscholastic Athletic Administrators Association and remains involved with his state association as the FIAAA's State Certification Coordinator.

Jake is also active at the national level having served as the Co-Vice Chair for the NIAAA's Certification Committee for several years and he has also presented workshops and taught LTI courses at the NIAAA Conference multiple times including again this year!

In June of 2020 Jake created the very popular **Educational AD Podcast** which showcases High School Athletic Directors, Authors, and other Educational Sports professionals from across the country. In addition, he is also the Director of Victory Educational Athletics which offers a wide variety of Professional Development programs and services to schools and organizations in the areas of Coaches Education, Athletic Leadership, and Parent Engagement.

Jake has been a featured speaker or presenter at numerous State, Regional, and National conferences on a variety of programs, but particularly on motivation and "Competitive Sportsmanship" a pre-season parent education series that has been adopted by dozens of schools across the country.

As a high school and college football and track coach, Jake was very successful, earning Coach of the Year honors 12 times in his career. Also, as a Health Educator, he was honored as the Outstanding College Health Educator of the Year for the state of Oregon, and he was a recipient of the NIAAA's State Award of Merit for Florida for his work in promoting Professional Development for Athletic Directors. You can reach Jake on Twitter at @jakestouchdown and email him at jakestouchdown@gmail.com

Made in the USA
Las Vegas, NV
25 September 2024

95795583R00066